# PRINCE2® in Action

## Project management in real terms

# PRINCE2® in Action

## Project management in real terms

SUSAN TUTTLE

**IT Governance Publishing**

IT Governance Publishing Ltd
Unit 3, Clive Court
Bartholomew's Walk
Cambridgeshire Business Park
Ely, Cambridgeshire
CB7 4EA
United Kingdom
www.itgovernancepublihsing.co.uk
© Susan Tuttle 2018

The author has asserted the rights of the author under the Copyright, Designs and Patents Act, 1988, to be identified as the author of this work.

First published in the United Kingdom in 2012 as Illustrating PRINCE2 by IT Governance Publishing.
ISBN 978-1-84928-325-0

This edition published in the United Kingdom in 2018 by IT Governance Publishing.
ISBN: 978-1-84928-980-1

# PREFACE

Using and understanding PRINCE2® comes as second nature to me. I am a born project manager and practitioner of the method in both my professional and private lives. That may sound strange, but that is how much I believe in this methodology. I see how it can be used and tailored to any project in any environment, at any time and with anyone – be it work-related or not.

On every training course I teach, I share my passion for PRINCE2 with my course delegates. By the end of each course, they love it, too. They understand the benefits and leave wanting to apply the methodology to their own lives (probably only their work lives, but that's still a start!). Now, I want to share this passion with you. My illustrations come from my own experience and from those people I've had the pleasure of working with over the years.

Please note: All names and places have been modified to protect the innocent, the naïve and the culpably disobedient.

*vi*

# ABOUT THE AUTHOR

Susan Tuttle has more than 20 years of experience in projects, programme and change management. She has a proven track record of producing exceptional results across diverse industries. She started her career in the financial industry in the US, before moving to IT consulting and earning her masters in training and development.

After moving to the UK in 2004, Susan became an accredited trainer in PRINCE2, MSP® (Managing Successful Programmes), Agile Project Management and change management. Her training style is influenced by her strong commitment to human development, which is continually demonstrated in her use of learner-centred adult learning theories and principles. She is an energetic self-starter with excellent analytical, organisational, and creative skills. She is committed to reaching out to project managers in need of advice, guidance, structure and empathy via project management conferences, social media, blog entries, podcasts and online training courses.

# ACKNOWLEDGEMENTS

I wish to thank my husband and best friend, Tony Leigh, for supporting me in my efforts to write this book.

*x*

# CONTENTS

Introduction...........................................................1
Example layout ...................................................1
Chapter 1: PRINCE2 Overview...........................3
Principles.............................................................3
Themes.................................................................5
Processes.............................................................6
Chapter 2: Seven Principles.................................9
Principle one: Continued business justification...........9
Principle two: Learn from experience.....................10
Principle three: Defined roles and responsibilities.........12
Principle four: Manage by stages.........................13
Principle five: Manage by exception ...................14
Principle six: Focus on products.........................16
Principle seven: Tailor to suit the project ...........18
Chapter 3: Seven Themes...................................19
Theme one: Business case .................................19
Theme two: Organisation...................................20
Theme three: Quality ........................................22
Theme four: Plans..............................................24
Theme five: Risk................................................26
Theme six: Change ............................................27
Theme seven: Progress .....................................29
Chapter 4: Seven Processes...............................33
Process one: Starting up a project......................33
Process two: Directing a project ........................34
Process three: Initiating a project......................37
Process four: Controlling a stage ......................39
Process five: Managing product delivery ...........41
Process six: Managing a stage boundary ...........43
Process seven: Closing a project........................45

# Contents

**Chapter 5: Starting up a Project ..................................49**

Appoint the executive and the project manager.............49

Capture previous lessons.................................................51

Design and appoint the project management team .........52

Prepare the outline business case ..................................54

Select the project approach and assemble the project brief
...............................................................................................56

Plan the initiation stage.................................................57

Tailoring guidelines .......................................................59

**Chapter 6: Directing a Project.....................................61**

Authorise initiation .......................................................61

Authorise the project......................................................63

Authorise a stage or exception plan ..............................65

Give ad hoc direction.....................................................67

Authorise project closure ...............................................69

Tailoring guidelines .......................................................70

**Chapter 7: Initiating a Project.....................................73**

Agree the tailoring requirements ...................................73

Prepare the risk management approach ..........................74

Prepare the change control approach .............................76

Prepare the quality management approach ....................79

Prepare the communication management approach .......82

Set up the project controls.............................................84

Create the project plan ...................................................86

Refine the business case..................................................89

Assemble the project initiation documentation (PID) ....90

Tailoring guidelines .......................................................92

**Chapter 8: Controlling a Stage.....................................95**

Work packages: Authorise a work package....................95

Work packages: Review work package status ................97

Work packages: Receive completed work packages ......98

Monitoring and reporting: Review the management stage
status .........................................................................100

# Contents

Monitoring and reporting: Report highlights ............... 102
Issues and risks: Capture and examine issues and risks 103
Issues and risks: Escalate issues and risks ................. 106
Issues and risks: Take corrective action ...................... 108
Tailoring guidelines ................................................. 110
**Chapter 9: Managing Product Delivery** .................**113**
Accept a work package ............................................. 113
Execute a work package ............................................ 115
Deliver a work package ............................................ 116
Tailoring guidelines ................................................. 117
**Chapter 10: Managing a Stage Boundary** ................**121**
Plan the next management stage .................................. 121
Update the project plan ............................................ 123
Update the business case .......................................... 125
Report management stage end .................................... 126
Produce an exception plan ........................................ 129
Tailoring guidelines ................................................. 131
**Chapter 11: Closing a Project** .................................**135**
Prepare planned closure ........................................... 135
Prepare premature closure ........................................ 136
Hand over products .................................................. 138
Evaluate the project ................................................. 140
Recommend project closure ...................................... 142
Tailoring guidelines ................................................. 143
**Chapter 12: Additional Suggestions and Procedures** .**145**
Business case theme: Relationships between outputs,
outcomes and benefits .............................................. 145
Organisation theme: Stakeholder engagement ............. 147
Quality theme: Recommended quality review technique
............................................................................... 149
Plans theme: PRINCE2 recommended approach to
product-based planning ............................................ 154
Plans theme: Product-based planning ......................... 158

## Contents

Risk theme: The risk management procedure...............161
Change theme: Issue and change control procedure.....166
Progress theme: Types of control ................................169
**Chapter 13: Tailoring PRINCE2....................................175**
Tailoring successfully ................................................175
**Chapter 14: Roles...........................................................181**
Project board ..............................................................181
Executive....................................................................182
Senior user .................................................................185
Senior supplier ...........................................................187
Project manager .........................................................188
Team manager............................................................190
Project assurance........................................................192
Change authority ........................................................194
Project support ...........................................................196
**Chapter 15: Management Products ...............................199**
Tailoring management products .................................199
Benefits management approach ..................................200
Business case .............................................................201
Change control approach ............................................202
Checkpoint report.......................................................203
Communication management approach.......................204
Configuration item record...........................................205
Daily log.....................................................................207
End project report .......................................................208
End-stage report .........................................................209
Exception report..........................................................210
Highlight report...........................................................212
Issue register .............................................................213
Issue report................................................................214
Lessons log.................................................................215
Lessons report ............................................................217
Plan ...........................................................................218

# Contents

Product description ..............................................219
Product status account...........................................221
Project brief.......................................................222
Project initiation documentation (PID)........................223
Project product description .....................................224
Quality management approach ..................................225
Quality register...................................................227
Risk management approach .....................................228
Risk register .....................................................229
Work package ....................................................230
**ITG Resources**................................................**233**

# INTRODUCTION

This book can be used as a guide to the PRINCE2 framework. It uses everyday language and everyday experiences. By providing a real-life context around the method, the translations and illustrations will provide evidence of how to use (and how not to use) the PRINCE2 method.

Each topic in this book is broken into three subsections. The first subsection will provide a basic background for the PRINCE2 subject under investigation. The second will translate that subject into layman's terms. Finally, an illustration will give further clarification and enable additional insight into the given area of project management.

**Example layout**

---

### PRINCE2 assertion

*This section will provide a brief summary or the basics of the method, as depicted in the PRINCE2 2017 Axelos guide. Each direct quote from the PRINCE2 guide will be represented in bold and italicised text to distinguish it from the author's text.*

---

*What this means*

This section will attempt to highlight key points from the PRINCE2 method to help the reader understand the meaning and context of the topic.

**Note:** For Chapter 15 ("Management products"), the "What this means" section is replaced with one entitled, "When is it created? When is it updated?".

## *Illustration*

This section offers a snippet, an example, or a story in real-world terms of people or companies using or misusing the PRINCE2 method.

**Note:** For Chapters 13 to 15 ("Tailoring PRINCE2," "Roles" and "Management products") a two-tiered illustration is provided, which shows how to tailor these aspects of PRINCE2 for small projects and large ones. Additionally, at the end of each Process chapter, sections are added to explain how the processes could be tailored based on their context - including simple projects, using an agile approach, or as part of a programme.

For a full, more in-depth explanation of the method and the best-practice references, please see the official Axelos product: *Managing Successful Projects with PRINCE2,* Axelos (2017).

# CHAPTER 1: PRINCE2 OVERVIEW

## Principles

---

### Overview

*PRINCE2 is principle-based rather than prescriptive, the principles are:*

- *Universal in that they apply to every project.*
- *Self-validating in that they have been proven in practice over many years.*
- *Empowering because they give practitioners of the method added confidence and the ability to influence and shape how the project will be managed.*

---

*The PRINCE2 principles provide a framework of good practice for people involved in a project and were developed from lessons taken from both successful and failed projects.*

---

### What this means

According to *www.businessdictionary.com*, guiding principles are defined as a "broad philosophy that guides an organisation throughout its life in all circumstances, irrespective of changes in its goals, strategies, type of work, or the top management." Principles in the PRINCE2 approach can be defined similarly. Seven underlying principles should be applied to every project, regardless of what is going on inside or outside the project environment. They are sound, proven rules, which can be used as markers on the way to project success.

## Illustration

By no means was Jermina's project perfect, yet she and her project management team received a company-sponsored award for excellence in project management. Jermina had followed the PRINCE2 principles throughout her project. She demonstrated the principles daily, which helped the project end on a successful note.

Decisions on her project did not have to come at a cost to the people and resources working on it. Instead, they were made objectively, with a concentration on confirming continued business justification (principle one). When new changes were required, no one took it personally. It either made business sense to include the change or to continue with the project without the change, depending on the impact on the business case. When things went horribly wrong, the manage by exception principle (principle five) enabled the team to get the right information to the right level of management, who could make an expedient and appropriate decision for the project. It worked like clockwork.

Everyone on the team was encouraged to learn from experience (principle two). With each issue, a lesson was captured and learned. Mistakes that were made were not repeated. On the other hand, positive lessons were always shared and frequently repeated. The team adhered to their defined roles and responsibilities, managed the project in management stages, and tailored the method to suit their circumstances. The focus on products principle (principle six) allowed all the team members to work creatively, so that they could contribute to and produce the best possible products – ones that were fit for purpose and supported the overall justification for the project.

For all their hard work and effort through all the ups and downs that come with managing a project, the team were recognised and rewarded by their company for sticking to the principles.

**Themes**

---

**Overview**

*The PRINCE2 themes describe aspects of project management that must be addressed continually as the project progresses through its lifecycle. However, the strength of PRINCE2 is the way in which the seven themes are integrated, and this is achieved because of the specific PRINCE2 treatment of each theme (i.e. they are carefully designed to link together effectively).*

*How the themes are applied can be influenced by tailoring. This may range from being rigid and prescriptive through to allowing the project management team a large degree of freedom as to how they implement each theme.*

*All seven themes must be applied in a project, but they should be tailored according to the risk, scale, nature and complexity or simplicity of the project concerned, always ensuring that any minimum requirements specified in a team are satisfied.*

---

*What this means*

Rules are not meant to be broken. Nor are they meant to be rigid, harsh and unyielding, regardless of the circumstances. They are meant to be helpful in allowing groups of people to get from one point to another without relying on gut instincts or worrying about personality differences, politics and/or conflicts. Themes in PRINCE2 introduce the idea of seven areas of project management that should be considered to set the right balance of rules (restrictions, constraints, limitations, controls, etc.), depending on the project's individual set of circumstances.

### *Illustration*

Have you ever played Monopoly according to the rules provided by Parker Brothers (the game's publisher) without any deviations? Either due to time restrictions, boredom levels or attention spans (these dependent on the immediate situation or the type, age, or size of the group playing), most people generate their own set of house rules for Monopoly. Some people put a time limit on the whole game and rule that whoever has the most money by the end of that time wins. Other players put limits on amounts to be borrowed from the bank, ensuring the faster demise of some of the players – and thus the overall game. Regardless of the reasons behind them, the house rules are there to suit the situation. They are agreed upfront and adhered to throughout the game. If they don't work for the players, they are adjusted with a group consensus, and the new set of house rules will then be used to finish off the game.

### **Processes**

| **Overview** |
| --- |
| *PRINCE2 is a process-based approach for project management. A process is a structured set of activities designed to accomplish a specific objective. It takes one or more defined inputs and turns them into defined outputs.* |

## *What this means*

Just as you don't bake a cake before you've mixed the ingredients, it is important to consider the separate activities involved in a project before starting it. The idea behind PRINCE2 processes is to give a sense of the natural order to the activities of a project. Some will have to be modified and adjusted according to the individual project characteristics, but the seven processes help provide guidance on what should be done and when, according to best practice.

## *Illustration*

An organisation reviewed a recently completed project to determine if it was worth the money they had invested in it. In order to conduct the review, the administration staff in the projects office were told to retroactively research the history of the project. They were to look specifically at what problem was being addressed, what options they had available at the time to deal with it – these options included the option that was finally chosen – and identify which of the benefits, if any, that are now being seen in the organisation can be linked to this effort.

According to the information uncovered, the project had gone over budget and over time and had only superficially addressed the original problem. Additionally, it had left the organisation with higher-than-anticipated operating costs to maintain the new solution. An attempt was made to retrofit the benefits, but no solutions were found. A second version of the project was then commissioned to fix these latest problems.

Wouldn't this assessment have been better placed at the beginning of the first project? A properly understood problem, approach and solution could have been identified and defined at the start of the project, instead of after, when it was too late. Somehow, there never seems to be enough time and/or money to start a project off well, but there's always enough to do it again!

# CHAPTER 2: SEVEN PRINCIPLES

## Principle one: Continued business justification

| PRINCE2 assertion |
| :---: |
| *A PRINCE2 project has continued business justification.* |

### *What this means*

Not only should a project be justified in its original expenditure commitment, but the reasons behind it should remain valid throughout the entire expenditure. If the reasons disappear, a decision should be made by management to continue at a loss or stop the effort.

### *Illustration*

A jilted bride, whose fiancé has recently dumped her for one of the bridesmaids, has a decision to make. She has already paid her deposit for the wedding hall. The reason for paying for the wedding was that there was going to be a wedding. The benefits of being a happy, loving couple starting out their lives together far outweighed the expense of hiring out the hall. Now that the wedding has been called off, does it make sense to continue to pay for it? It depends, of course.

If the bridegroom had dumped the bride one year or more before the wedding, the bride could have recouped her deposit without any penalty fees. If it had happened six months prior to the wedding, the bride may have lost the deposit, but could still cancel without having to pay the full price. However, what if the bridegroom's disappearing act occurred on the wedding day itself? All the costs would already have been spent, but none of the original benefits would be realised. Is it still worth having the reception party, even without the groom? Sounds like this matter might need to be escalated to corporate, programme management or the customer (perhaps the father and/or mother of the bride? Or family attorneys?)

**Principle two: Learn from experience**

| **PRINCE2 assertion** |
| --- |
| *PRINCE2 project teams learn from previous experience: lessons are sought, recorded and acted upon throughout the life of the project.* |

### *What this means*

This assertion centres on the idea that we should take time to review and reflect on past experiences to make future ones easier, faster and better. If we jump too fast into the doing of a project – without looking back at what has been done before – we will either be doomed to repeat our mistakes or to recreate the wheel every time we start something new.

### *Illustration*

Six years ago, company X found itself in a situation where its headquarters was the only office that had access to and control of any of the company policies. Satellite offices in other locations complained they could not tailor work to suit their local needs. A project was immediately put in place.

Three years later, the new chief executive officer (CEO) at the headquarters office inquired about the set of policies and procedures used at the organisation to fully understand the work being done around the world. No one could provide a full set, as each satellite office had its own way of recording and documenting procedures. The new CEO immediately put in place a project to centralise all the records – including all the policies and procedures – to capitalise on a streamlined system of operating.

Today, at the annual board meeting, managers from the satellite offices complained of being oppressed and manipulated into using a set of stringent and inflexible procedures that were irrelevant to their specific local and regional needs. And the story continues.

Advice for company X would be to implement the learn from experience principle immediately. First, they would need to reflect on previous projects and the reasons behind them. Is the company stuck in a cycle of repetitive change for the sake of change? Sometimes, projects can be used to distract management away from more fundamental problems within the organisation. If it is determined that this latest move to centralise (or decentralise) is truly required in the current circumstances facing the organisation, then the organisation must reflect on what went well and what went badly during the previous. In other words, the company must use its previous experiences as a benchmark to improve (in terms of project management competencies and maturity levels, at the very minimum).

## Principle three: Defined roles and responsibilities

---

**PRINCE2 assertion:**

*A PRINCE2 project has defined and agreed roles and responsibilities within an organisational structure that engages the business, user and supplier stakeholder interests.*

---

### What this means

For every job, there is a portion (hopefully not a huge one) that is considered boring. Nobody likes doing the boring stuff. If we had our choice, we'd only do things that were fun. But if everyone only worked on the fun stuff, none of the boring stuff would ever get done. The defined roles and responsibilities principle ties into the importance of assigning the right task to the right role and the right role to the right person/people. This way, everyone will be clear on what they are signing up to do, and get the opportunity to work on both the fun and the boring portions of the project.

### Illustration

Everyone knows that a football (soccer) team has 11 players on a pitch at any one time. Each player is responsible for their position. If players started to play in different positions willy-nilly, then there would be 11 strikers and no keeper. Everyone would be stepping over each other trying to get to the goal. With too many cooks in the kitchen, so to speak, there'd be no one playing defensively, and the opposing team would have an easy time scoring.

Every player on the team needs to know where they should be playing and where the others should be, at all times. That isn't to say that a defensive player can't take advantage of a lucky breakaway and run the ball up the pitch towards the goal. If that were to happen, at least one of their teammates would stay behind to cover their position. Everyone would feel confident that the pitch was being properly manned.

**Principle four: Manage by stages**

| |
|---|
| **PRINCE2 assertion:** <br><br> *A PRINCE2 project is planned, monitored and controlled on a stage-by-stage basis.* |

*What this means*

Can you predict the future? No one can with any guarantees. The best one can do is take a best guess at what you think the future will hold. But that is all it can be: a best guess. If one were to take a best guess about the details of the next five years, they would undoubtedly get it incredibly wrong. Even if you had every fact and figure from all that had happened in the past, you could never accurately predict details of the future. Instead, a better option would be to take a stab at prejudging the details of the near future and provide a broad, best-guess picture of the long-term future.

*Illustration*

Jenny knew she wanted to travel for a year after graduating from university. She would use the trip as a reward to herself for completing her degree. She used this goal as a focal point to get her through the doldrums of studying and revision sessions. However, with more than two years to go, she could not, with any certainty, predict the exact details of what flight she would take, how many days after graduation she would leave, or any of the minute details about her trip. Instead, she broke her plans into manageable steps, which she dealt with one by one, in the buildup towards her sabbatical.

When she finally stepped on the plane for the first leg of her trip, she had all the right visas and all the right vaccinations. If she had planned these details at the beginning – three years ago – she would have had the wrong ones. Visa and vaccination requirements are constantly changing with the times and events of the world. Luckily, she planned the details for these only at the management stage (the final step) where they were needed and could be predicted with accuracy.

**Principle five: Manage by exception**

---

**PRINCE2 assertion:**

*A PRINCE2 project has defined tolerances for each project objective to establish limits of delegated authority.*

---

*What this means*

Senior managers take on a lot of responsibility when they sign up to the project board. However, they can't usually afford to dedicate more than a minimal amount of effort and time to complete a project. Rather, they rely quite heavily on the project manager to control the day-to-day management, while they continue to run their departments or directorates and continue to attend the innumerable meetings required of them. So, how do they take ownership of something that they don't execute themselves? They delegate power down to the project manager in the form of change authority and tolerances. Change authority is the delegated responsibility for the consideration of changes, while tolerances are the permissible deviations from a plan's target(s).

If the project manager is working within their agreed authority levels, they are allowed to get on with the work. The project manager is required to provide periodic progress reports to prove they are operating with their limits. If a situation takes them outside of these limits, they must immediately escalate the situation – also known as an exception situation.

***Illustration***

When a new project manager is delegated a management stage with zero tolerances and zero change authority, this might indicate that the project board either does not trust the project manager, or does not have confidence in them. However, if after several successful management stages the project board still will not relinquish any stage-level tolerance and/or change authority, then the project manager may infer one of two very likely scenarios. Either the project board members still do not trust them, or they are a tyrannical band of micromanagers. They will want to appear to delegate responsibility for the project one management stage at a time, but really, they are ensuring that they are heavily involved in absolutely every decision that deviates from the stage plan. With even the tiniest of issues pulling the project manager outside their stage-level tolerance, or the most inconsequential of change requests being above their change authority, every issue or change becomes an exception – which requires an exception report and, thus, the project board's involvement.

On the other hand, when a project manager is being delegated an enormous amount of stage tolerance, it does not indicate that the project board has copious amounts of trust in them. It is more likely that the project board members understand the time pressures of their other commitments (running a department or sponsoring other change initiatives, for example) and recognise that they may not have a lot of time to give to this project. Thus, with excessive amounts of stage tolerance, the project manager is bound to be able to stay within their limits and, therefore, will not need to interrupt the project board with exceptions.

## Principle six: Focus on products

---

### PRINCE2 assertion:

*A PRINCE2 project focuses on the definition and delivery of products, in particular their quality requirements.*

---

### *What this means*

It is easy, and often natural, for people to start planning out a piece of work by focusing on what activities are required to get the work done. However, with a focus on the activities and the journey, it is easy to go off on a tangent away from the desired end goal: the finished products. Principle six asserts that attention must be given to the products every step of the way as, otherwise, it becomes easy to lose sight of what is important and get caught up in the politics, obstacles and unnecessary details of the result.

## 2: Seven Principles

### Illustration

Allison really wanted a bicycle for her birthday. She mentioned it, dropped hints and gave obvious signs that this was what she desired. Eventually, her husband, Andrew, finally 'heard' her and started the ball rolling.

He spent hours on the Internet researching road bikes, mountain bikes for off-road riding, and trick bikes for freestyle jumping and stunts. He decided on mountain bikes because of their superior safety features. He then spent his lunch hours, Saturday mornings and a few evenings looking at and testing mountain bikes. He invited Allison's friend, Mary, to help him choose between the two he liked best. Mary was of a comparable size and shape to Allison, so her input was essential. When, at last, he had decided on the type, size and colour (Allison's favourite, of course), he ordered it. It was to be delivered on Allison's actual birthday, so it could be a surprise.

If only Allison had been clear about her expectations from the beginning, and not relied on clandestine clues. Getting a new bike was one of her birthday wishes, of course, but spending time with her husband was what she really wanted. The bike was merely a means to an end. She had her heart set on the experience of the two of them perusing over new bikes, finding the one that spoke to them both, and possibly even buying two, so they could ride together and spend even more time together. Instead, she got herself an absent husband who'd been spending more time with her close friend than he had with her, and a heavy cardboard box on her doorstep (with no card!).

## Principle seven: Tailor to suit the project

| PRINCE2 assertion: |
| :---: |
| *PRINCE2 is tailored to suit the project's environment, size, complexity, importance, capability and risk.* |

*What this means*

A one-size-fits-all strategy rarely works for anything, much less large investments in project work, which are inherently unique and different from other work. Principle seven requires the project management team to consider the special characteristics of each project and tailor PRINCE2 – a best practice framework – to fit the needs of the project, rather than to force the project to fit PRINCE2.

*Illustration*

A dressmaker, commissioned to make one bridal gown (size-12) and one dress for the maid of honour (size-16), is expected – if not required – to tailor the dresses to suit the separate measurements of the two women, rather than to create two size-14 dresses (the average size of the two women). Additionally, the gowns need to be of different fabrics, colours and complexities. The bride, wanting to wear a white, floor-length gown, should not be upstaged by her maid of honour, also wearing a white, floor-length gown.

# CHAPTER 3: SEVEN THEMES

## Theme one: Business case

| Purpose |
| --- |
| *The purpose of the business case theme is to establish mechanisms to judge whether the project is (and remains) desirable, viable and achievable as a means to support decision-making in its (continued) investment.* |

### *What this means*

The business case sets out the case to the business. "Please give us (the project team) your money today, and we will create products that will result in benefits in the future," would be a business case, for example. It may seem that businesses must take a gamble on one project idea over all the others. But with solid research, diligent fact-finding, and careful financial assessment, the gamble can also be seen as taking a calculated risk.

### *Illustration*

Over the last few years, politicians have been trying to persuade the general public that the solution to our pending electricity shortages is nuclear power. They show us pages and pages of facts and figures demonstrating the huge benefits of nuclear power (which include increased supplies, supply as and when we need it, and its ability to cope with growing demands – especially when oil runs out) mapped up against the costs – which are relatively low, even with maintenance and waste costs included. The one thing they don't tend to focus on – even though it's pretty much the only thing we, their constituents, can see – is the risk! One fault, one mistake, one accident and we, the constituents, may not be here anymore.

A good business case maps out all three aspects: the expected benefits, the costs (including ongoing sustainable costs) and the risks to give you the true story. It will also be updated periodically to prove that the continued expenditure against the effort is still worth it – what if a completely safe alternative energy source were discovered halfway through the project?

## Theme two: Organisation

---

### Purpose:

*The purpose of the organisation theme is to define and establish the project's structure of accountability and responsibilities (the 'who'?).*

---

### *What this means*

When lines of reporting are clearly drawn, and people know whom they are to report to and who is to report to them, they can concentrate on how to get the work done. If these essential lines have not been clarified, then people will either be frightened into inaction – not knowing if they have authority to act – or end up stepping on each others' toes, each person thinking they have the authority over the other. Either way, conflict and chaos normally ensue.

### *Illustration*

Bill and Annie belonged to the same gym. They regularly ran into each other there after work, and sometimes at the weekends. Back at work, Annie was a financial expert working as the team manager for a major project. Bill was the executive of that project. After work one night, Annie bumped into Bill at the gym and told him of a concern she had earlier that day about some of the figures she was working on. She was going to call Bob, the project manager, the next day, but since she and Bill were both at the gym, she let him know about the problem there and then. When Bill went home that night, he started working remotely, investigating the problem, crunching numbers and sending email after email to try to find a solution. He worked long into the wee hours of the morning to no result.

The next morning, Bill showed Annie his work, and they reviewed the numbers again. Both Bill's and Annie's administration staff were helping by pulling up old databases, perusing old spreadsheets, and dusting off old accounts. No one was getting any closer to the solution. Finally, some time around lunchtime, in a desperate call Annie phoned Bob, the project manager. She asked him if he had access to an old record on a latent database that she thought might have some clues. Confused by her request, he enquired about her reasons. Annoyed and frustrated, Annie said that she didn't have time to explain, and gave a rushed response about the situation.

Alarm bells went off in Bob's head. This shouldn't be happening! He asked her which version of the data she was using for her calculations. It turned out she had been using data from a different project and hadn't realised it. So, when all the numbers hadn't added up, she'd suspected fraud or negligence.

If either Bill or Annie had informed the project manager of the issue (as would have been required, so the project manager could capture them in the issue register), then none of this time and frantic effort would have been wasted! Skipping reporting lines can only hurt the project. If the project manager is unaware of an incident, there is no way they can even attempt to control it.

## Theme three: Quality

> ### Purpose:
>
> *The purpose of the quality theme is to define and implement the means by which the project will create and verify products that are fit for purpose.*

### *What this means*

The quality theme expresses the need to collaborate with the customer to define the quality expectations and measurable acceptance criteria. A full understanding of what is required will help the team plan how they can do their work to meet their objectives. Without knowing the 'what', planning out the 'how' will be impossible. Either too much or too little will be done, and this can lead to many undesired disputes. If too much is done, the costs will seem extravagant. If too little, the project risks non-acceptance from the customer.

The quality theme goes on to ensure that what has been defined and agreed is actually being built and tested, according to the definitions and agreements. Every output is fully defined in a product description, which indicates exactly the minimum criteria the product must meet to be accepted. The project team can then figure out exactly how much work and effort it will take to produce that level of quality. Their plans will reflect that effort and they will manage against those plans. Managing quality then becomes an everyday pursuit: pervasive in every aspect of the project and not just an afterthought.

## Illustration

Maria hired Damien, a party planner, to organise her husband's 50th birthday party. She gave him a list of her ideas for the party, which covered the size, theme and type of venue. She felt her ideas were clear, unambiguous and complete. She knew exactly what she wanted. The first thing Damien did, however, was to go through Maria's list with her to ensure that he fully understood her ideas, asking for clarification in measurable terms. The party was to be a black-tie event for 300 of their closest friends and family, and held in a five-star venue. Once he had fully understood, Damien built his plans to ensure that the quality Maria was asking for was what she would get.

Damien's plans included working with Maria to define the specific criteria she required for each element of the party, such as the invitations, decorations, music and menu. Each item was defined in detail, so that when items were purchased or booked for the party they met the exact requirements (the quality criteria). The plans also included quality-checking throughout the project. Each required and defined item needed to be tested. As Maria was busy, she asked her son, Alberto, to be the official tester.

Maria approved the plans, as they showed Damien would be doing the right type and amount of work to create the party she wanted. As agreed in the plans, Alberto did the venue walkthrough before the contract was signed. He did the taste testing of the menu before it was finalised. He also approved the decorations, the music list and the invitations – all according to the acceptance criteria already defined.

The attention to quality from the start to the end ensured Maria was satisfied with the end result. She was more than happy to sign off her acceptance at the end, and gave Damien a glowing recommendation. Sometimes, a focus on quality can get a bad name as something that is labourious, hard to do, and too slow. Yet, in reality, it is actually less work, easier and faster to implement a quality product.

## Theme four: Plans

| Purpose: |
|---|
| *The purpose of the plans theme is to facilitate communication and control by defining the means of delivering the products (the where and how, by whom, and estimating the when and how much).* |

### *What this means*

PRINCE2 plans are designed and directed at specific audiences. Because there is a potential for three levels of management in a PRINCE2 project management team, there is a potential for three levels of plan for a PRINCE2 project. The top-level plan is the high-level view of the overall project. The project board are the key audience here, they get enough information about the current predictions and estimates for the whole project. The second level is for the project manager. It represents a shorter space of time – a management stage – within the project, and provides enough detail for the project manager to maintain day-to-day control over the work. Then, if there are team managers on the project management team, they may want and/or be required – as detailed in the terms of the work package – to create a team plan. This plan allows the team manager to stay on top of the work – typically complex in nature, if not in size – carried out by the team members below them. Each plan has its own use and, thus, provides just enough information.

### *Illustration*

In front of Jo sit three sheets of paper. On them are three different lists representing her plans and goals for running her life. Each list contains a different level of detail to help her manage her time and effort effectively.

The first is her to-do list (i.e. the team plan). After work, she must pick up the dry-cleaning on her way home, meet her friends out for dinner, and leave a message for the neighbour about sweeping his front garden. The level of detail here allows her to execute her tasks for the day with precision and accuracy.

The second sheet is her monthly calendar (i.e. the stage plan). She has listed on it her appointments, meetings and events on the appropriate dates. Most entries are noted with the exact time, such as the 9am dentist appointment, while others are noted with more flexibility, such as the picnic on Saturday the 16th. The information here allows Jo to manage and control her time on a day-to-day basis.

The final sheet of paper is Jo's list of 100 goals to accomplish before she dies (i.e. the project plan). She has listed things like climbing the pyramids, sailing a boat, seeing the Grand Canyon, swimming with dolphins, etc. She has predicted the year or decade for when she would like to complete each of these goals, as well as listed ideas on how to accomplish them. The level of detail here allows her to manage how and when she will achieve her life goals by showing the major products, activities and resources required.

## Theme five: Risk

| **Purpose:** |
| :---: |
| *The purpose of the risk theme is to identify, assess and control uncertainty and, as a result, improve the ability of a project to succeed.* |

### *What this means*

Projects cost money. The amount of money they cost is usually compared with the benefits they promise to achieve and the amount of risk they could present. A tricky project decision to make is how much of the project budget should be spent on mitigating risks. The organisation's attitude towards risk, the executive's attitude towards risk, and the team's attitude towards risk all need to be included in this consideration. The more money spent on risk-mitigating activities, the less money is then available for getting the project work done. However, if no (or very little) is spent on managing risks, a culture of blame can ensue with, "I told you so" quickly becoming the project motto.

### *Illustration*

Here is a project management conversation overheard from one end of a telephone:

"Yes, you're right. A meteorite may hit the Earth and have quite a devastating impact on my project. So, how much of my project budget should I allocate against mitigating the risk that a meteorite may hit the Earth?"

... Pause ...

"None, you say? Why's that? If the risk does come to pass, my project may potentially cease to exist. That seems like a pretty significant risk to me!"

... Pause ...

"So, you're saying it's because of the probability. I must match impact against the probability to gain a true understanding of the size of the risk."

... Pause ...

"I guess you're right. According to NASA and the other institutions who monitor the skies, the probability is infinitesimal: so small, that even when mapped against the huge impact, the overall size is *very, very low!*"

... Pause ...

"OK, then. It makes sense that I will not spend one penny managing this risk. I will accept it in full and continue to monitor."

## Theme six: Change

| Purpose: |
| :---: |
| *The purpose of the change theme is to identify, assess and control any potential and approved changes to the baseline.* |

### What this means

Just because someone comes up with a great idea halfway through a project – long after the project definition work has been completed and agreed – does not mean we will not include it. However, we will only include changes that make sense. To determine if a change makes sense, an assessment must be completed for each and every change request. Based on the assessment, a determination needs to be made by an authorised party within the project management team to include, reject or defer the request. If the decision is to include the change, it must be paid for. This can be from the change budget, additional funding or even at the cost of de-scoping other areas of the project.

### *Illustration*

A client calls the office. The project manager is out. The team member working on the client's product is in. They talk. Though they've met once or twice before at social events, all their project communication tends to go through the project manager but, as previously stated, he's stepped out of the office.

The team member listens to the client and takes on board his request for a "teeny-weeny" change. Since he is already working on the product, it would be no problem for him to add the change. And there it is: scope creep.

It can happen as simply as that; a seemingly small change is requested and accepted without any formal documentation or authorisation. It's easy – the team member is currently working on the product, he has all his tools out, and he is finishing things up. A tiny change would be no problem. Or so it seems.

A whole slew of problems can arise from such a transaction. Either that 'tiny' change will end up taking the team member five times longer than he expected, or the new change will have knock-on effects on other products, which will then also need to be changed. Another possibility is that the client will forget that they requested the change and will not accept the final product because it does not meet the documented requirements. In any of these scenarios, the scope of the project increases without the appropriate time and budget to deal with it being allocated. Even small changes require time and budget expectations to be reset. If there is a change budget to pay for changes, time expectations will still need to be reset.

**Theme seven: Progress**

---

**Purpose:**

*The purpose of the progress theme is to establish mechanisms to monitor and compare actual achievements against those planned; provide a forecast for the project objectives and the project's continued viability; and control any unacceptable deviations.*

---

*What this means*

Plans are based on estimates, which, by definition, can only be approximations, best judgments or calculations. However, to know what activities should be done and when, a plan is usually required. Plans in project management are used as tools to help control the work of the team and to measure the team's progress. Progress information will indicate if the work is going according to plan, or if new or different measures need to be brought in to better control the work.

Just because an estimate – or best guess – in a plan says that an activity will take two days, does not mean it will actually take two days. Plans need to be monitored and updated with facts and dates in order to determine if the desired and agreed level of progress is happening. Each level of management in the project management team will use the plans as an aid to complete and monitor the work, as well as a tool to help bring unexpected situations back into the agreed timeline.

### *Illustration*

Jessika is working on a fairly large and complex project. One of her team managers is a highly skilled scientist with years of experience. Ten days ago, she authorised a work package to him and he accepted it. Ever since, his team of scientists has been busy at work.

The deadline for the work package is fast approaching and Jessika has no idea if the products will be completed on time. She has no idea because of her own mistake. She decided that regular progress reports (checkpoint reports) were not required for this work package, since she did not have the scientific background to understand the nature of the work. Now, looking in from the outside, all she sees are extremely busy scientists spending hours and hours in labs, working late into the night. Is this what is supposed to be happening? It would have been better to have agreed to some form of progress updates than to live in limbo, waiting and observing frantic behaviour that may or may not be normal for this type of work.

A project manager needs to know where the project is at any given time. "Where are we now?" could be the project manager's mantra. Or, even better, "Are we within tolerance?" Progress data from the team managers needs to be captured and compared with the estimates in the plans. Issues need to be captured and assessed against the plans for their impacts. Change control needs to be invoked to assess the impact of changes against the plans.

# CHAPTER 4: SEVEN PROCESSES

## Process one: Starting up a project

| Purpose: |
| --- |
| *The purpose of the starting up a project process is to ensure that the prerequisites for initiating a project are in place by answering the question: do we have a viable and worthwhile project?*<br><br>*The purpose of the starting up a project process is as much about preventing poorly conceived projects from ever being initiated as it is about approving the initiation of viable projects.* |

*What this means*

To trigger a PRINCE2 project, someone with enough authority from within an organisation needs to commission the project idea. The project idea is presented as a project mandate – either formally as a written document, or informally as a verbal request. Regardless of presentation, the idea is still just an idea. Even if it is a wonderful idea, it may be that it is not possible to execute – perhaps due to the organisation's existing time and resources, or because it's not sustainable, or maybe because business conditions have changed and the idea is no longer valid. The starting up a project process ensures that bad ideas are not pursued, and good ideas are understood before they are initiated.

The project board will need information about the project idea before they commit resources to its initiation. A high-level investigation will determine answers to these basic questions about the project's viability, logistics and resource commitment.

## *Illustration*

A group of old friends meet up in a pub. They sit around a table, catching up on each other's lives. They realise how much they miss each other, and start talking about spending more time together. Someone invariably suggests going on holiday together. The gang, together again, rally round the idea. Already, they are talking about the best times of the year to go, and where to travel.

Promises are made, but not kept. Some friends won't be able to afford it. Some won't get the time off work. Others, still keen on the idea, won't be able to agree on the basics – such as the type of holiday (i.e. the business options), or whether to use a travel agent or book it themselves (i.e. the project approach).

Just because someone has an idea doesn't mean it's a good one. Just because it sounds like a good idea in theory doesn't mean it will last the test of time. Ideas need to be poked at, tested, reviewed and considered. If they are worthy and viable, they can be pursued in earnest. If not, they'll do it all over again at the next pub meet-up.

## Process two: Directing a project

| Purpose: |
| :---: |
| *The purpose of the directing a project process is to enable the project board to be accountable for the project's success by making key decisions and exercising overall control while delegating day-to-day management of the project to the project manager.* |

## What this means

Directing a project is a process reserved for the project board. In this process, project board members make scheduled and unscheduled decisions. Their scheduled key decisions are made at the start of the project, at the end of the project, and at the end of each management stage. Their unscheduled decisions are normally made at times where the project manager is forecast to exceed their tolerances, as laid down by the board. They can also be at any other time. Board members can pick up the phone, email, or communicate otherwise with the project manager at any point in time. This is called "giving ad hoc direction." It is advisable for the project manager to record such ad hoc direction in writing – possibly via email – so that the content and its significance is not later misconstrued or devalued.

## Illustration

As Jim approached Fred in the corridor leading to the open-plan office, Fred had an overwhelming sense of dread. However, it wasn't until Jim started talking that Fred truly understood this odd emotional reaction.

"Fred, I'm glad I caught you. I've just been asked to take on this project and, when I was thinking of who could be the project manager, I immediately thought of you. You are perfect for this."

Jim spoke on and on in elated tones. Fred stopped listening. He'd been here before. In fact, three times before. When Jim's enthusiasm reached a feverish pitch, Fred snapped.

"As long as it won't be like before!" he almost yelled in a very loud, stern tone.

"Huh? Uh, what do you mean?" Jim responded, completely stunned.

"Well, let's see," Jim continued, as he regained his composure. "The last three projects on which we 'worked together,' I was left completely on my own ..."

*(Authorise initiation – confirm that all members have agreed roles.)*

"... One was a complete disaster, and only stopped when Maria (the internal legal consultant) advised the corporate management team of the nebulous legal grey areas we were fast approaching ..."

*(Authorise the project – confirm that there has been a review of the risks.)*

"... The second finished all right, but I am now not on speaking terms with more than half of the customer service department ..."

*(Authorise project closure – ensure that the appropriate groups have been made aware of their responsibility for taking any recommended actions forward.)*

"... And the third technically finished six months ago, but the client just called me asking for my latest progress report."

*(Authorise project closure – review and issue a project closure notification.)*

"So, if you really want me to project manage this new project, I need things to be different. I'm all for the management by exception principle – it lets me get on with my job without being micromanaged – but 'management by complete and utter absence' is not fair. It's not fair to me, the team or the customer! If you can accept my terms, then

I'm on board but if you can't, then you'll need to find someone else."

"I'll let you think about it," added Fred, confident things would be fine. He returned to his desk and updated his daily log with notes on their conversation, just in case.

## Process three: Initiating a project

---

### Purpose:

***The purpose of the initiating a project process is to establish solid foundations for the project, enabling the organisation to understand the work that needs to be done to deliver the project's products before committing to a significant spend.***

---

### *What this means*

If a project is to progress smoothly, it needs to have certain criteria defined upfront, an agreed set of rules to abide by, and a plan to work against. The initiating a project process puts these details in place by focusing the time and attention of the project management team on deciding and agreeing to the terms of the project before the actual specialist or technical work begins. If the terms and conditions can be agreed, then there is a better chance of them being adhered to during the actual work. If there are issues or concerns with agreeing the terms, then the specialist work should not commence until these have been negotiated and finalised. There is nothing worse than starting a project under the pretence that 'we' will figure it out as we go. That only leads to disaster and, more likely, strained relations with everyone involved. There will no longer be a 'we,' just an 'us' and a 'them', even after the project dies a painful death.

### *Illustration*

Salima pulled out her stage plan for the initiation stage and began to laugh. When she had first started using PRINCE2 several years back, she had the false impression that the initiation stage was all about the project manager busily documenting a bunch of bureaucratic documents for the sake of bureaucratically documenting documents. If only the 'Salima of a few years back' could see her initiation stage plan today. How eye-opening it would have been.

Salima's schedule had her attending meetings, running workshops, conducting presentations, delegating pieces of work, checking on progress, reviewing drafts, and even producing a bit of documentation. It takes a lot of input, negotiation, facilitation, persuasion and – in some cases – mediation, for the project management team to establish the foundations for the project. Although the project manager is responsible for producing much of the documentation in the initiating a project process, they must work with a lot of other resources to get it right.

In her case, Salima was working with an entire team of expert users to help her define the quality criteria for all the products that were being planned for. She was also holding planning workshops with team managers to ensure that their input and expertise was considered, as well as to confirm their availability and commitment to carry out the team manager role. She was having regular meetings with project assurance to review the information sets being defined for the project. She even had a few presentations to deliver to key stakeholders, in order to maintain their level of support and interest in the project.

All of these activities were planned for in the initiation stage plan and authorised by the project board in the "authorise initiation" step *(see* Directing a project*).* Everyone on the project board realised that this amount of effort was required to define the project and garner support and agreement. The project initiation documentation (PID) resulting from this stage will form the 'contract' between Salima and her project board. It is in everyone's best interest that this is done correctly: with the right levels of involvement from the right resources at the right times.

## Process four: Controlling a stage

| Purpose: |
|---|
| *The purpose of the controlling a stage process is to assign work to be done, monitor such work, deal with issues, report progress to the project board and take corrective actions to ensure that the management stage remains within tolerance.* |

### *What this means*

Just as an orchestra's conductor is authorised to conduct and direct a musical piece (not the complete works) of a composer, a project manager is authorised to manage a management stage (not the entire project) on behalf of the project board. In keeping with this analogy, the orchestral conductor has the music sheets in front of them, assisting the aid of their direction to the appropriate musicians and their instruments. The project manager uses the stage plan and work packages to steer the work of the team managers.

And finally, the conductor of an orchestra – as the group's focal point – not only directs the music, but handles the issues (personality conflicts, for example) and wards off the risks (of mistakes). The project manager uses the risk and issues registers to help control the management stage.

### *Illustration*

Mark is the project manager. He sees himself as a spoke in the wheel. The flow of information up and down the project goes through him. This is how Mark remains in control. He takes direction from the project board and delegates work out to team managers. When team managers have issues, they raise them with Mark. If those issues are indeed exceptions (exceeding stage-level tolerances), then Mark escalates them to the board.

Before Mark started the management stage, his stage plan was reviewed, examined and authorised by the project board. The project board was fully aware of the products and activities Mark intended to handle, and approved him for them. Mark uses this stage plan on a daily basis to instruct him on what to do next. Some days, he needs to authorise work packages; other days he needs to review progress and send highlight reports. As his current management stage is drawing to an end, he has noticed that soon he will need to start planning the next management stage (via the managing a stage boundary process). Today, however, he is to review his risk and issue registers. He is chairing the risk workshop in the morning, in which the risk owners and risk actionees will report their progress and brainstorm further ideas. Later in the day, he has reserved time with the project support team to review and update the statuses of several recent issues that have been resolved.

## Process five: Managing product delivery

| Purpose: |
| --- |
| *The purpose of the managing product delivery process is to control the link between the project manager and the team manager(s), by agreeing the requirements for acceptance, execution and delivery. The role of the team manager(s) is to coordinate an area of work that will deliver one or more of the project's products. They can be internal or external to the customer's organisation.* |

### What this means

Project managers may be good at managing projects, but they don't necessarily have the skills to do the specialist work on it; hence, the need for the team manager role. Team managers have the requisite skill set to do or manage the specialist work. Depending on the size and nature of the project, there may be several team managers working on different aspects or products for the project. However, if the project is small in nature or size *and* the project manager also has the requisite specialist skills, there may be no need for additional people to fulfil the team manager role. Regardless of the situation, the work must still be agreed on, executed and handed back to the project. The mechanics of how this is done must be agreed in the work package. Beyond that, the mechanics of the specialist work is left to the specialists under their agreed terms and conditions.

### Illustration

*Question: Who's a better project manager? Jacques or Jackie?*

Jacques used to be a high-level techie, and was able to find solutions when no one else could. He works hard, learns all the latest methods, has all the latest gadgets, and is always willing to stay late to help finish tasks. He has always been a significant asset to any project team.

Jackie has never been a techie. She knows people, however. She's supervised and managed up to hundreds of staff members through times of recession, expansions, mergers and downsizes. She is excellent at managing people through change, as well as getting the most out of them.

The answer to the question is: it depends. However, it does not depend on if the project is technical in nature. The best project manager knows how to manage. The name is in the title; a project manager will allow a team manager and team members to get on with the specialist work, stepping in only to help them manage the work, not do it.

If Jacques, as project manager, steps in to help bring the team back on track by doing techie tasks, he is taking his eyes off the project he is supposed to be managing, and repositioning himself as a team member. If the team is falling behind, Jacques, as project manager, will need to help manage the situation: remove obstacles, find opportunities, resources and answers.

However, if Jackie is clueless about the technical nature of the project, and can only manage the situation, she might be relying on specialists who take her project down a path that is unrecoverable. If she allows the specialists full reign over all the decisions – and doesn't understand the impacts of them – she may lock the project and/or the business into solutions that are not sustainable.

**Process six: Managing a stage boundary**

---

**Purpose:**

*The purpose of the managing a stage boundary process is to enable the project board to be provided with sufficient information by the project manager, so that it can review the success of the current management stage, approve the next stage plan, review the updated project plan, and confirm continued business justification and acceptability of the risks. Therefore, the process should be executed at, or close to the end of, each management stage.*

*Projects do not always go to plan and in response to an exception report (if the management stage or project is forecast to exceed its tolerances) the project board may request that the current management stage (and possibly the project) is re-planned. The output from re-planning is an exception plan, which is submitted for project board approval in the same way that a stage plan is submitted for approval.*

---

*What this means*

After each management stage completion, the project board will make a key decision about the project. Either they will continue to fund the project by authorising the next stage, or they will request a premature close. To make such a monumental decision, the project board requires up-to-date and accurate information. Without it, they could potentially make the wrong decision. Therefore, it is important for the project manager to gather the most up-to-date information about the project, its progress and its continued viability. Once it has been presented to them, the project board members will be able to make the appropriate and informed decision that best suits the needs and interests of the business, the users and the suppliers. Similarly, if the project board requests that the management stage or project be re-planned based on an exception situation, the project manager will need to present the most up-to-date information about the project, especially about the impact of the exception on the project.

### *Illustration*

In the film *Austin Powers: International Man of Mystery* (1997), Dr Evil, a villain who had been cryogenically frozen for 30 years, unfreezes and wants to hold the world hostage in an evil plot for the sum of one million dollars! 30 years is a long time to go without information. The world changes so quickly these days; six months can be a long time to go without information.

The project board will get to decide how far into the future they want to go before they stop and assess and decide if they want to continue with a project or not. At each of these stopping points – often called "end-stage assessments" – they will need up-to-date and accurate information about the current situation as it currently stands – not from six months ago, for example, when the original business case and project plan was written. Thus, the project manager is tasked with researching and gathering this data towards the end of every management stage in the managing a stage boundary process. Of course, the project board will receive regular highlight reports detailing the progress of a management stage during its execution, but the end-stage assessment concerns more than just progress. It is a full assessment of the progress made to date, but also includes revised predictions for the future and a confirmation of continued viability – all of which is required to determine whether to carry on with the project or to stop.

## Process seven: Closing a project

| Purpose: |
| --- |
| *The purpose of the closing a project process is to provide a fixed point at which acceptance for the project product is confirmed, and to recognise that objectives set out in the original project initiation documentation have been achieved (or approved changes to the objectives have been achieved), or that the project has nothing more to contribute.* |

### What this means

After a project ends, most of the project management team members will move on to other projects or back to their old jobs. Regardless of where they move on to, they leave the project in their past. If users have questions about the project's products after a project has closed, it is often difficult to find anyone who had worked on the project to ask. Even if they could be found, it would be unlikely that they would remember enough of the details and intricacies to be able to answer a usability question.

One of the major objectives of the closing a project process is to ensure that users are provided with all the relevant information available to use, operate and maintain the project's products. If a usability question arises after the project has finished, they will be able to answer it themselves. Additionally, this process ensures that the project has not only passed on ownership of the outputs, but also the lessons from the effort (i.e. the lessons report), the completed documentation of what actually happened (i.e. the complete, updated and archived documentation) and a complete assessment of the effort and its success (i.e. the end project report).

### *Illustration*

At Janie's previous company, there wasn't really a process to properly close a project. When they were done with the specialist products, they would turn off the old version and turn on the new one. There was always an extensive list of new project ideas to be started. The pressure to quickly (and sloppily) hand over the current project outputs and start working on the new ones was immense. Senior management at her old firm knew this was a problem, but continued to support the lack of any proper handover process to keep moving forward with the creation of new products.

The results of this approach were disastrous. The users were unhappy with the products. Because the users either didn't use the products or misused them, the benefits that had justified the project were not realised. As Janie was the project manager who introduced the new outputs, her name was associated with them. She received endless phone calls from the operational teams asking how to maintain or manage different outputs. With the high-speed turnaround of projects, rarely did she remember the specifics of any one output among the many she churned out.

When Janie joined her new company, she was elated to hear that the use of PRINCE2 was embedded in the organisation.

When planning for the final stage of her project, Janie relished the opportunity to finally plan it and do it right. She looked forward to being able to review a final product status account to confirm that the project's products had been approved and met their quality criteria. She couldn't wait to confirm acceptance from operations and maintenance organisations, and transfer the responsibilities for the products to them. She was excited to finally do a proper evaluation of a completed project: to review the original and current version of the project initiation documentation, assess the project against the expected benefits in the business case, and review the team performance. And lastly, she was delighted by the idea of working with the project management team to prepare a lessons report, in which she would reflect on the experience and really learn from what had gone well and what had gone badly.

# CHAPTER 5: STARTING UP A PROJECT

## Appoint the executive and the project manager

| Description: |
| :---: |
| *To get anything done in the project, a decision maker with appropriate authority is needed – the executive – who represents the interest of the business stakeholder(s). The appointment of the executive is a prerequisite to ensuring that the project is justified.* |
| *The appointment of a project manager allows for the project to be managed on a day-to-day basis on behalf of the executive. The executive may need to consult with, and gain agreement from, corporate, programme management or the customer when appointing a project manager.* |

### *What this means*

To get the project idea off the ground, a member of management with enough seniority, interest and authority will need to be appointed. This person will own the project, but will rarely have enough time to dedicate to doing it. Therefore, they will appoint a project manager. The project manager will do the legwork. They will research the idea and work with stakeholders amongst others (including the executive) to gather high-level information on which a decision to start the project or not can be based. The project manager should be trusted by the executive, as their skills will be required to bring the project to successful completion – adding yet another triumph to the name and reputation of the executive.

## *Illustration*

James was tapped on the shoulder by his boss and asked to sponsor the project idea just announced at the company meeting. Understanding that he was taking on the role of the project board executive and accepting total accountability for the project, James turned around and tapped Julia on the shoulder, asking her to be the project manager. Having worked on several projects before in the past, James and Julia were comfortable taking on these roles. James's role description was produced by the corporate management team above him. Once he had gained a firm understanding of his authority levels as an executive on the project, James could advise Julia on where her authority levels below him would lie. She then drew up her role description with these limits in mind.

Although this was a small project within the overall organisation, it was important for James and Julia to document the differences between their roles. James would be the decision maker for the project, and Julia the planner and doer. This clear line of authority was now not only clear to them, but also to all the stakeholders affected by the project work. James could spend his time managing his directorate, promoting the project idea and advising Julia. Julia could spend her time getting on with managing the project, stage by stage.

## Capture previous lessons

> ### Description:
>
> *A number of lessons may have been learned by other projects, corporate, programme management or the customer, and external organisations about weaknesses or strengths of the processes, procedures, techniques and tools used, when they were used, how they were used and by whom.*

### What this means

Although you might have just been presented with a seemingly brilliant idea about the future, one of the first activities should be to look back into the past. Imperative questions need to be asked and answered before taking the idea any further. Has anything like this project ever been attempted before? If so, what can we learn from that experience? What went well that we could repeat? And what mistakes were made that we can avoid? If nothing like this has been done before, why not? Did others think of it and decided not to pursue it? What was their reasoning? What threats did they foresee that we might be missing? Can we address those threats and still turn this into a positive experience?

### Illustration

Considerations are being made to include a visitor centre in the terminal building in PortCity during their next big refurbishment project. Never having been involved in setting up or even managing a visitor centre, no one in the organisation could provide any insight into how best to go about doing it. One of the administrator's old neighbours had worked at the Hall of Justice in RiverCity a few years back, when they opened their visitor centre. The project manager looked the neighbour up and met with him to discuss his experiences. The project manager asked the neighbour what went well during the project and what he would have done differently if he had had the chance to do it over again. From this interview, the project manager gathered several key ideas on how best to go about the project, where the risky areas might be, and possible starting points.

The neighbour gave the name and number of someone who had helped him when he started his project. This second contact was also from PortCity, and potentially had even more information and lessons learned about the local clientele, public reactions and climate. Although the RiverCity project went well, the dynamics could have been different in PortCity, so another interview was set up.

**Design and appoint the project management team**

| Description: |
| :---: |
| *The project needs the right people in place, with the authority, responsibility and knowledge to make decisions in a timely manner. The project management team needs to reflect the interests of all parties who will be involved, including business, user and supplier interests.* <br><br> *It is essential for a well-run project that every individual involved in the management of the project understands and agrees who is accountable to whom for what, who is responsible for what, and what the reporting and communication lines are.* |

# 5: Starting up a Project

## What this means

For very small, simple projects, many of the PRINCE2 roles can be combined, reducing the need for a large number of people in a situation that does not call for it. For example, the executive and senior user, who both come from the customer organisation, can often be combined. Additionally, the project manager can fulfil the roles of project support and team manager. However, the larger or more complex a project is, the more need there will be for more people to be involved. Some roles may even need to be shared by more than one person (for example, there could be more than one senior user, multiple team managers and a project support team). However, for the roles of executive and project manager, there should only ever be one person.

## Illustration

Duane and Birthe worked together on a small project. After they had reviewed lessons from previous small projects, they realised they could combine roles. Previous projects, to which a lot of people had been added, ended up being slower and less efficient than other projects for which the team had been kept to an absolute minimum.

Duane then planned to fulfil three roles: those of the project manager, the team manager and the project support. He would not have to assign himself work packages, nor create team plans, but he would have to switch between focusing on how the management stage was progressing and focusing on the specialist work at hand. He would also have to be very diligent in maintaining his own administration.

Birthe planned to tackle both the roles of executive and senior user, as well as retain both business and user assurance responsibilities. She appointed a senior supplier from the supplier organisation to fulfil the roles of senior supplier and supplier assurance. Birthe could have informal project board meetings via phone and emails with the senior supplier, whenever needed. To satisfy her assurance roles, Birthe arranged to hold regular mentoring and review meetings with Duane. And finally, Duane and Birthe split the change authority role – with Duane taking authority on all changes worth up to £500, and Birthe taking the authority for anything worth more than £500. Their design was documented in an email, and the role descriptions were filed in a project folder.

### Prepare the outline business case

| Description: |
|---|
| *When setting up, and particularly while running the project, it is all too easy to concentrate on what is being done and how it is to be done, while ignoring why it needs to be done. Given the information available, the outline business case is likely to be only a high-level view at this time. It provides an agreed foundation for a more extensive business case developed in the initiating a project process.* |

*What this means*

The executive, in consultation with the senior user, if appointed at this time, should be drafting the outline business case, especially capturing information about objectives, reasons, and business options associated with the project idea.

Meanwhile, the project manager will be consulting with the executive, the senior user and the senior supplier to capture early opinions and ideas about the expectations and acceptance criteria associated with the project idea. They should also be capturing any risks associated with these findings on the daily log. Because it's only early days with the idea, there may not be much detailed knowledge available. Only enough information to formulate a decision about the project idea's viability is required (this depending on the project idea concerned).

### *Illustration*

Based on your own experience, expertise and understanding of the following, decide, at a high level, if these are good or bad ideas:

- Creating a company website
- Upgrading the existing IT infrastructure
- Changing working practices of the front-line staff
- Conducting a staff audit
- Moving company headquarters to a different building
- Outsourcing the company help desk overseas.

Depending on your situation, you may or may not be able to make a case for one or more of these actions. If you cannot make a case, even at a high level, you should not start the project.

**Select the project approach and assemble the project brief**

| Description: |
|---|
| *Before any planning of the project can be done, decisions must be made regarding how the work of the project is going to be approached. An agreed project brief ensures that the project has a commonly understood and well-defined start point.* |

### What this means

A project brief is just that: brief. Although there are several key sections to consider and possibly document, the overall aim is to keep it as brief as possible. The project brief is created during the pre-project preparation and, thus, is only an early opportunity to explore the idea at a high level. The aim is to find a feasible way to execute the project. One that still provides the users with an acceptable end product, while giving the business enough benefits to make it worthwhile.

### Illustration

A husband and wife are considering how best to go about a DIY project (what approach to use). Jason believes that, if he wants something done right, he should do it himself. Jason has some limited experience in crafting things from scratch. He not only has a clear vision of what he wants, but the drive and determination to complete what he starts. He also has the time to do it, which counts as free labour for this project.

Meghan, his wife, doesn't quite agree. She feels that, if you want quality work done, you must pay professionals to do it. Her experiences and previous lessons tell her that Jason's perceptions of his own craftwork are not quite the same as hers. She either has to live with taps installed backwards, walls painted the wrong colour, and doors that open out instead of in, or pay someone to fix them after Jason has finished. She would rather use professionals from the start – ones who can use their years of experience and possibly some sort of a qualification or degree. Not only will they get what they want, but it will be exactly right the first time.

Together, Meghan and Jason took time out to evaluate their options. They considered other changes that were going on in and around their household, such as the impending birth of their first child and the major road works going on in their neighbourhood. They considered the quality standards they would want the DIY project to meet, and the safety and security constraints that would be required with the new baby. At the end of the discussion, they agreed to hire in professionals. The cost/time/risk assessment of this option proved it was the best approach for delivering the desired outputs, as well as achieving the outline business case. Once agreed, they could then assemble the project brief.

**Plan the initiation stage**

| **Description:** |
| --- |
| *Initiating a project takes time and consumes resources. The work should be planned and approved like any other project work. This also ensures that the initiation is not aimless and unstructured.* |

## What this means

The work and effort required to create and document the project initiation documentation needs to be planned out. The plan for this initial stage should be at a stage plan level, allowing the project manager to maintain day-to-day control over it. Typical activities shown in the plan may include such things as workshops, meetings, drafts, consultations and reviews. All of these will need to be funded and resourced. The only way the project board can allocate enough time and resources for this stage is if it is clearly presented in the plan.

## Illustration

Sean (the project manager) and Julie (the executive) were in a rush. Thus far, they had informally discussed all the aspects of the small project idea. In their dialogue, they felt that they had exhausted the activities outlined in the starting up a project process. Sean believed he was ready to move to the initiating a project process. Julie gave him the nod to proceed. The only thing missing from their conversation was the detail about how the initiation stage would be run. Sean assumed he would fit the initiation stage work around his other business as usual duties. Julie believed that he would drop everything to complete the initiation. After a week, Julie expected Sean to return with at least a draft of the PID, so they could pick up their conversations about the project and start agreeing on some of the basics. When she called him in, it turned out he hadn't even started.

Even in a very informal implementation of the starting up a project process, it is important to agree on the time, money, effort and resources required to do the next step, the initiation stage.

**Tailoring guidelines**

| Description: |
| :---: |
| *The activities in this process may be combined, split or run concurrently to suit the context, but care should be taken to ensure the integrity of the interface with the directing a project process when a request to initiate a project is submitted.* |

*What this means*

This process is performed pre-project. Because of this, not all of the information and resources may be in place yet. For example, the end result of the project may not be known, but the business problem that needs to be solved or the desired outcome from the project should be. The project manager may not be in place, as this project may not get the official 'go-ahead', the process then defaults to the executive and any persons they appoint to complete the process on his/her behalf.

*Illustration of common situations*

- **Starting up a simple project**
  Elijah met with his boss, the executive, to talk through an upcoming project idea. Their meeting lasted roughly two hours, but they covered everything - from why they needed the project, what the project would accomplish, who would be involved, how they'd go about it, etc. At the end of the meeting, Elijah's boss asked him to summarise their discussion in an email, so that she could reply with her confirmation that they would officially move into initiating a project process, next.

- **Starting up projects using an agile delivery approach**
  Ellen's main concern in starting up a project process was her company's inexperience with using an agile method. To-date only two staff members had participated on an agile project, and both of those were at different companies. As part of the starting up a project process, she held an early workshop with key stakeholders to discuss the pros and cons of using an agile method and to ensure that all the right preventative measures were put in place to make it work.

- **Starting up projects from a supplier perspective**
  Alexandra received a request for proposal from a potential customer. She began the starting up a project process to ensure that this project would provide enough of a return. If at this early stage, it was determined the investment would not be worth it for her company, she would not submit the proposal.

- **Starting up projects within a programme**
  Christopher was asked to be a project manager for an upcoming project at his company. Instead of invoking the starting up a project, he and the rest of his team were invited to a workshop run by the programme manager. Information was shared, questions were answered and clarifications made. At the end of the meeting, it was clear that Christopher and his team's next steps were to perform the initiating a project process.

# CHAPTER 6: DIRECTING A PROJECT

## Authorise initiation

| Description: |
| --- |
| *Projects take time and cost money to initiate, so the activities for initiation should be planned, monitored and controlled. The project board activity to authorise initiation ensures that such investment is worthwhile.* |

### *What this means*

*Decision: Is this project idea worthy of further investigation?*

Once an idea that is at least worthy of a second (more detailed) look has been discovered, a request will be sent to the project board to authorise initiation. This decision publicly shows commitment to the organisation and other senior managers. In essence, the project board is saying, "This idea has been deemed worthy of further investigation. If the project manager comes around to bother you or your staff, it probably has to do with this project, and they have our permission." By making this decision, the project board does not commit itself to the entire project, as only a few key pieces of information have been researched to date. However, through their public commitment to resourcing the stage plan for initiation, they demonstrate their enthusiasm for the initial findings thus far.

## Illustration

How do you know if you have enough information to determine if the idea for a project is worthwhile? In 1962, Decca Records didn't think the Beatles had the right sound for the times. In 1977, Digital Equipment Corporation didn't feel that there would be enough people interested in having a personal computer in their homes. In 1999, Excite didn't see the value of buying Google for one million pounds.

These, of course, were famous bad business decisions that turned out to be wrong ones. Taking these decisions is difficult. PRINCE2 allows monumental decisions like these to be broken down into two steps. This helps to prioritise work, gain clarity, and understand total commitment and investment. The first decision is to decide to only investigate further, rather than rely on high-level information to make a decision. Once the investigation is completed and the details sorted, then another decision can be taken to commit to the project (*see* Directing a project, *Authorise the project).*

How different the world would look if all major investment decisions were approached like this! Western Union might have bought the telephone patent for £100,000. Atari or Hewlett-Packard might have hired Steve Jobs and Steve Wozniak without their college degrees, instead of competing against them. And the Coca-Cola Company may have purchased the then-bankrupt competitor and rival Pepsi in 1931.

## Authorise the project

| **Description:** |
| :--- |
| *This activity will be triggered by a request from the project manager for authorisation to deliver the project, and should be performed in parallel with authorizing a stage or exception plan. The objective of authorising the project is to decide whether to proceed with the rest of the project.* |

### What this means

*Decision: Now that we see it in detail, do we really and truly believe in this project idea?*

The completed PID will contain all the details of what the project is to achieve, who will be involved, how it will be run and managed, and why it is needed in the first place. Using the PID as an objective tool, the project board will then need to decide if they are still committed to the idea. Now that they see it in detail, will they publicly commit to the project for a second time? This time, their decision will indicate to the rest of the organisation and other key stakeholders that the project idea is now not only viable and worthwhile, but desirable and achievable.

### Illustration

Carlos – the project board executive – was, along with the rest of his board, about to take the decision to authorise a project. This project was to be the biggest the company had ever taken on in its history. The project board had previously agreed, in principle, to the project through an informal onsite meeting (*authorise initiation*), but now was the time to declare commitment and investment, or prematurely close it down.

To eliminate distractions, Carlos hosted an offsite meeting with the project board members, where they could review, discuss and approve the project, or not. He wanted the decision they made to be the right one. Carlos also insisted, as a prerequisite for attending the meeting, that all project board members and/or their designated project assurance resources had reviewed and assessed the project's lesson log, PID and benefits management approach. If they were to discuss this project in detail, the details had to be known and understood beforehand.

For where there were contentious areas – especially between the senior users and the senior suppliers – rational discussions were held, negotiations – where necessary – were made, and resolutions were found at the senior management level. As a result of this meeting, the common level of understanding and deep level of commitment that Carlos sought was achieved. This fundamental point in the project would set the precedence for the level of engagement required from the project board for this specific project. When the decision was made at the end of the day, they were all certain it was the right one.

**Authorise a stage or exception plan**

| Description: |
|---|
| *It is important that a management stage starts only when the project board says it should. The project board authorises a management stage by reviewing the performance of the current stage and approving the stage plan for the next stage. Approval of stage plans occurs at the end of every management stage except the last one.* |
| *If an exception has occurred during the management stage, the project board may request that the project manager produces an exception plan for project board approval.* |

*What this means*

*Decision: Do we stop here, or continue on?*

Even though the project board has authorised the project in a separate decision, they only agree to commit to funding and resourcing the project one management stage at a time. At the end of each management stage, they must again agree to continue or to prematurely close it down. To make such key decisions, the project board requires up-to-date and accurate information from the project manager. An updated project plan and business case will prove the project is still worthwhile and achievable. The next stage plan will show the details of the next proposed work needing funding and resources. And finally, the end-stage report proves that the current management stage has been successfully completed, and the team is ready to move on to the next stage.

If the project board is meeting to review an exception plan, then it was they who requested to see one. When a project manager is predicting to exceed their stage-level tolerances, then they must first raise an exception report. The report explains the situation and provides a number of options, including the project manager's recommended option. As long as the situation does not take the project board outside of project-level tolerances, they are free to make any decision they wish. They could fix the problem for the project manager, they could request the project prematurely close, or they could request to see an exception plan. Usually, the project board will want to see one of the options suggested from the exception report in more detail in the exception plan (hopefully the recommended option). If requested through the 'give ad hoc direction' action, then the project manager uses the managing a stage boundary process. They would create the exception plan, update the project plan and business case, and document an end-stage report providing an assessment of the management stage up to the point of the exception situation. This information would then be used to assess whether to continue with the project or not. Like at the natural end of a management stage, the project board uses this up-to-date information to determine if the project, at this point, is worth continued investment to recover from the exception or if they should prematurely close it down.

### *Illustration*

Deborah's project was almost complete. She had one more scheduled management stage to do, which mainly focused on adding nice-to-have functionality to her existing project's products. She had just performed the managing a stage boundary process, in preparation for the end-stage assessment with the project board. The board held these meetings in person to provide a specific time and space to hash out any concerns and answer questions before authorising a stage. In this particular meeting, where Deborah wanted the final stage to be authorised, the project board was divided. Some members wanted to cut and run, while the others wanted to stick it out to the end. For the ones wishing to end prematurely, the last stage did not convince them as being worth the effort. The sooner the project resources could be released back to their business as usual, the better; in their opinion, the project had gone on long enough. However, other members wanted to continue to the end to give the team the satisfaction of completing the effort. By cutting them off before the end, it might destroy or severely damage their morale. In the end, the decision was made by the executive, who limited the discussions after everyone had had their chance to voice their opinions. He decided to continue as planned for the final stage.

**Give ad hoc direction**

| **Description:** |
| --- |
| *Project board members may offer informal guidance or respond to requests for advice at any time during a project. The need for consultation between the project managers and the project board is likely to be particularly frequent during the initiation stage and when approaching management stage boundaries.* |
| *Ad hoc direction may be given collectively or by individual project board members.* |

## What this means

*Decision: Do I/we pick up the phone to the project manager (or email, smoke signal, Morse code them, etc.) and give solicited and/or unsolicited advice?*

If the project board, or even just a member of the board, is communicating with the project manager outside of the end-stage assessments, they are performing the 'give ad hoc direction' action. They may do this because the project manager has requested some advice, or because the project board member(s) has/have a question for the project manager. Either way, it is always a good idea to record these ad hoc conversations, emails, or phone calls and their results.

## Illustration

Will, the senior user, stopped Katerina in the hallway with a question about the project she was managing. The following day, Naomi, the project board executive, emailed Katerina. Later, she received a phone call from the senior supplier, asking for a quick clarification of the highlight report.

Although these communications with the project board members were on informal terms, Katerina kept a record of each of them in her daily log and, where appropriate, in the project documentation too. The senior user's question was really a request for change on one of the existing products, and Katerina started the change control procedure by capturing it on the issue register. The executive's email was really an update on a threat that she owned. Katerina updated the risk register and continued with the risk management procedure. The five-minute explanation to the senior supplier was only noted on her daily log. Although it only took five minutes, this was the third time it had happened. If a trend was to arise from this, she may solicit informal advice about a potential change to the communication channel through which the senior supplier receives his highlight reports.

## Authorise project closure

| **Description:** |
| :-- |
| *The controlled close of a project is as important as the controlled start. There must be a point when the objectives set out in the original and current versions of the project initiation documentation and project plan are assessed. Without this approach, the project may never end; a project can become business as usual and the original focus on the benefits will be lost.* |

### *What this means*

*Decision: Is it over?*

It's not over until the project board says it's over. The project board will want to see evidence before confirming the project closure – evidence that the products have been completed, tested and approved; evidence that the products, remaining issues, risks and the benefits management approach have all been handed over; and evidence that the project has been evaluated and lessons learned and shared.

### *Illustration*

All that was left for Joaquin to do now was to click "send" on the project closure notification email to his project stakeholders. He had received the draft project closure recommendation from Evie, the project manager, confirming that the project was ready to close. The project assurance resources had helped him review and assess the project initiation documentation, the end project report, the lessons report and the benefits management approach. The project had delivered its objectives and had nothing left to contribute. Any ideas for future enhancements (follow-on action recommendations) for future projects or continual improvement efforts were captured and shared with the appropriate groups. The handover of the project's products was successful and deemed sustainable. The business case had been scrutinised, reconciling the expected costs with the actual costs and identifying which benefits had actually materialised and which were still to be realised. The arrangements for resourcing the remaining benefits listed in the benefits management approach had been confirmed and agreed.

As the executive – the ultimate decision maker on the project – Joaquin did it. He hit send. Project stakeholders were then informed they could withdraw their support and infrastructure resources, as well as being notified of the closing date for costs to be charged against the project.

**Tailoring guidelines**

| Description: |
| --- |
| *After approval to initiate the project has been confirmed, care should be taken to ensure the integrity of the interface to the initiating a project, managing a stage boundary and closing a project processes when the formal decision to start the next management stage or close the project is made.* |

> *The degree of formality may differ in different circumstances provided decisions are explicit and traceable, ranging from verbal advice and decisions to those which are formally documented in email, meeting minutes or other traceable formats.*

## What this means

The accountability for this process lies with the executive, though the activities are normally performed by the entire project board. The project manager presents information to the project board to take these decisions, but should not take on the role of decision-maker.

## Illustration of common situations

- **Directing a simple project**
  Caleb's project only lasted two management stages - the initiation stage and the remainder of the project. His interaction with the project board was minimal and informal.

- **Directing projects using an agile delivery approach**
  Ava acted as the senior user and executive of an agile project. She had to reorganise her working arrangements and work schedule to ensure she was available to the project at a moment's notice. If and when project decisions were required, she needed to ensure they were made quickly and efficiently, as part of the agile ethos. She ensured that she attended all the demonstrations and retrospectives held to stay on top of progress and direction of the project, so that when decisions were required, she'd have first-hand knowledge and experience to react accordingly.

- **Directing a project from a supplier perspective**
  Henry was one of several senior suppliers on the customer's project. Because his company contributed a big chunk of the technical expertise for the project, he was made a member of their project board. He also acted as the executive for the project on his own internal project board, ensure that viability of the company's involvement with the project.

- **Directing a project within a programme**
  As programme manager, Lucia decided that for two of the projects in the programme she would also act as the executive. The first project was a critical one, where the entire rest of the programme relied on its success. She decided to be more involved rather than delegating this to someone else to champion and direct. The other project was extremely small compared to all the others. It didn't quite warrant the overhead of a project board. The project manager could report straight to her.

# CHAPTER 7: INITIATING A PROJECT

## Agree the tailoring requirements

| Description: |
| --- |
| *The project manager may need to tailor how the project is directed and managed in order to recognise internal and external factors that affect the way in which the project is delivered. Any deviations from the organisation's standard project management approach must be documented and agreed.* |

### *What this means*

Tailoring is a central aspect of a PRINCE2 project. It is, therefore, important to consider and agree how tailoring will be incorporated and managed throughout the project from the very beginning. Some organisations have existing tailoring advice through a projects management office (PMO) based on size, type and complexity of the project. In other organisations without centralised project management functions, the project manager will need to explore options for modifying the approach to fit with the circumstances of the project. Lessons learned from previous projects are a great source of information of what went well and what didn't.

### *Illustration*

Delila's company did not have any pre-existing, documented advice on how to tailor PRINCE2 for her project. So, she took it upon herself to find previous projects of comparable size and complexity, in order to garner lessons from how they adapted PRINCE2. Unfortunately, previous projects either did not fit the similar profile or hadn't used PRINCE2. She then did some research online to uncover ways of tailoring that had been tried in other companies. She found a few white papers that helped and took these findings to the executive. It turns out the executive had been involved with a similar project at her previous company, so was also a wealth of information. Together they discussed ways to combine roles and adapt documentation to fit the needs of the project. Delila presented these ideas to the rest of the project board for confirmation before commencing with the rest of the initiating a project process.

**Prepare the risk management approach**

| Description: |
| --- |
| *The risk management approach describes the goals of applying risk management, the procedure that will be adopted, the roles and responsibilities, the risk tolerances, the timing of risk management activities, the tools and techniques that will be used, and the reporting requirements.* |

*What this means*

*Consideration: How will this project team manage risks?*

The project management team needs to decide how they want to manage risks before they can start to manage them on the project. Each project will be different, not only because of the people involved, but the size and nature of the project. Some organisations will have strict risk management guidelines, while others may not have any. Additionally, partnership projects will need to investigate the best method for the project: theirs, ours, or a combination of the two?

Sample considerations:

- How risk-averse is the organisation and the project board?
- How will risk management be delegated throughout the project management team?
- How will risks be captured? In a Microsoft® Excel® spreadsheet or a database?
- How will risks be analysed and assessed? Using a risk model or software?
- How will risks be rated? What scales will determine a "high," "medium" or "low" rating?
- How often should risks be reviewed and reported?
- How will the team respond to risks? Using PRINCE2 responses or corporate standards?
- How much risk are they willing to live with?
- How much money should be set aside to deal with risks?

### *Illustration*

Tommy reviewed the corporate risk management strategy for the construction company he worked for. Most of the risks and the guidance related to catastrophic risks, health and safety standards and regulatory guidance. Tommy's project was about hiring a design firm to launch a marketing campaign. Nothing in the existing corporate documentation mentioned risks regarding advertising, reputation or commerciality. Tommy would have to start almost from scratch to create the project's risk management approach.

As a result of working with the project board, members of the project assurance team, and the design firm, Tommy's end result was a well-prepared and somewhat cautious approach. The project board's appetite for risk was fairly low, so they set the risk tolerance levels for the project quite low. Based on that decision, Tommy put a strict risk management procedure in place and recommended a fairly large risk budget. Risks were to be reviewed twice weekly by the project manager and project support. Weekly risk reports were to be provided to the project board and the design firm's senior management team. Project assurance was to perform monthly reviews of the procedures. A quarterly audit was scheduled to ensure adequate risk management in accordance with the approach.

**Prepare the change control approach**

---

### Description:

*Change control is essential for the project to maintain control over its management and specialist products.*

*The level of control required will vary from project to project. The maximum level of control possible is determined by breaking down the project's products until the level is reached at which a component can be independently installed, replaced or modified. However, the level of control exercise will be influenced by the importance of the project and the complexity of the relationship between its products.*

---

### *What this means*

*Considerations: How will this project team manage its products and control change?*

The project management team needs to decide how they want to control the project's products before they can start to manage the project. Each project will be different – not only because of the people involved, but the size and nature of the project. Some organisations will have strict change control guidelines, while others may not have any. Additionally, partnership projects will need to investigate the best method for this project: theirs, ours, or a combination of the two?

Sample considerations:

- How will change control activities be performed on this project, and by whom?
- How will records be kept, stored and accessed?
- How will issues and changes be captured?
- How often will records be reviewed, audited and reported?
- How often will change control activities be performed?
- How – if needed – will the change authority function of the project board be delegated within the project management team?
- How will issues and change be prioritised?
- How much money will be set aside to manage change?
- How will decisions on changes (requests for change and off-specifications) be made?

## *Illustration*

In deciding how they were going to manage the project's management and specialist products, Sandra and her team had to define their approach to change control. They were lucky that their organisation – the International Management Journal Network (IMJN) – had clear and well-defined procedures in place for projects that had documents as their main outputs. From years of doing projects that produced recommendation papers, research articles and case studies, the organisation had developed excellent tools and techniques to identify, track and protect documents, ranging from draft forms to final versions.

Sandra's project was to design and host a massive marketing event to coincide with their company's upcoming 10-year anniversary. Some of the products that were to result from the project did include some documents, such as the invitations, guest list, seating chart and contracts with suppliers. These could follow the organisation's current standards. However, a lot of the specialist products for this project would include things such as marketing gadgets and giveaways for their guests. Decisions needed to be made on how to identify these gadgets and gizmos, where to store them, and how to protect them against theft or damages until the big day. Storing these physical products on the company's document management system would not be appropriate.

In the end, Sandra and her team cleared out a space in one of the company's storage cupboards in the basement. When the physical products were completed and delivered to the site, they were stored under lock and key until they were needed at the event itself. A strict change control process was put in place and the senior user acted as the project's change authority, deciding on all requests for change. A sophisticated asset management system was used to track the different decorations (banners, signs, balloons and booths) and giveaways (pens, toys, t-shirts, digital clocks, magnets, handheld tablets, smart phones and memory sticks). Using this system and staying on top of all change requests, the team remained in control of the outputs. On the actual day, the venue was decked out to perfection, and every attendee walked away with the right promotional toys and giveaways.

### Prepare the quality management approach

| Description: |
|---|
| *A key success factor of any project is that it delivers what the user expects and finds acceptable. This will only happen if these expectations are both stated and agreed at the beginning of the project, together with the standards to be used and the means of assessing their achievement. The purpose of the quality management approach is to ensure such agreements are captured and maintained.* |

### *What this means*

*Consideration: How will this project team manage quality?*

The project management team needs to decide how they want to manage quality before they can start to manage it on this project. Each project will be different, not only because of the people involved, but the size and nature of the project. Some organisations will have strict quality management guidelines, while others may not have any. Additionally, partnership projects will need to investigate the best method for this project: theirs, ours, or a combination of the two?

Sample considerations:

- How will quality planning be conducted?
- How will quality be controlled? What quality standards need to be adhered to?
- How will quality be recorded, verified and reported, and how often?
- How will quality checks be conducted, and the results documented?
- How will products be tested and approved?
- How will quality assurance activities be conducted, and how often?
- How will quality management be delegated throughout the project management team?

Thinking about quality at the end of a project is usually too late. Many projects fail because most of the time and energy is spent in the production of products and waiting to see if they pass a test at the end. If at this point they don't pass, it's normally too late or there isn't enough budget to fix the problems.

For every project, it needs to be determined how the quality of the products will be proved. It will always depend on the type, size and nature of the products being produced. It will also depend on the degree to which quality needs to be proven. If regulatory bodies are insistent that certain tests are conducted and passed in order for the product to be "certified," then those will need to be included in the decision of how the products will be tested. If the user wants guarantees of safety, then safety checks will need to be included.

These tests will need to be planned and resourced. Objective testers will review and determine if the product(s) meet the desired criteria. Objectivity is key in testing for quality. If the creator of a product tests it, there will be reason to doubt the validity of the test. The very human temptation to pass your own work can sometimes override the goal of impartial judgment for a test. Robot arms and crash test dummies, however, have the disadvantage of not being able to pass personal judgments. When human resources are involved in testing, it is best to use people who are not involved or connected to the production, so they can remain objective. These additional resources are not normally cost-free for the project, so planning for their time and costs will need to be built into the project's plans and overall budget.

### *Illustration*

Refrigerator door manufacturers use mechanised robot arms to open and shut refrigerator doors up to 1,000 times in a row to prove that the suction around the door will still work properly.

Car manufacturers set up mock crash sites and use crash test dummies to prove their quality.

IT developers hold user acceptance testing sessions on new systems to prove that they are usable and intuitive for their target audiences.

Food manufacturers run taste tastes and trials to prove a new product's appealing taste and market interest.

For safety reasons, certified professionals are employed on construction projects. In order to prove the weight-bearing capacity of foundations, they use complex, specialised machinery to conduct dynamic load tests.

Children's toys manufacturers are required to comply with multiple international safety criteria for their toys, which are tested by certified testers – normally adults – to prove their safety.

Drugs manufacturers test their products in a number of different ways – with laboratory experiments, animal testing, and even human testing – before claiming their safety for the general public.

If none of these types of tests apply to your products, then how far will you go to prove their quality? What is your reputation worth?

**Prepare the communication management approach**

---

### Description:

*The communication management approach addresses both internal and external communications. It should contain details of how the project management team will send information to, and receive information from, the wider organisation(s) involved with, or affected by, the project. In particular, where the project is part of a programme, details should be given on how information is to be fed to the programme.*

*If a formal stakeholder engagement procedure is needed, this should also be documented as part of the communication management approach and should record the types of stakeholder, desired relationships and key messages, strategies for communication, and methods for evaluating the success of communications.*

---

## *What this means*

*Consideration: How will communication both within the project management team and with other stakeholders be managed?*

The project management team needs to decide how they want to manage communications before they can start to manage it on this project. Each project will be different, not only because of the people involved, but the size and nature of it. Some organisations will have strict communication management guidelines, while others may not have any. Additionally, partnership projects will need to investigate the best method for this project: theirs, ours, or a combination of the two?

Sample considerations:

- What communication methods will be used, and how?
- What communication tools will be used, and how? (For example, newsletters, email, site visits, road shows, podcasts, etc.)
- How will communication records be kept and referenced?
- How will feedback from stakeholders be captured and managed?
- How will communication be reported, and how often?
- How will communication management be delegated throughout the project management team?
- How will stakeholders be analysed?
- How will this project interface with programme communication management requirements?

## *Illustration*

Judy's programme management team had already devised a fairly extensive communication management approach. She was to follow the guidelines defined, as they were pertinent to her project. Due to the delicate nature and importance of her project to the programme, sensitive and considerate communication was required. The programme management team had, therefore, decided that all communication activities with external stakeholders would be conducted by them. No one on the project management team could discuss this project or their efforts with anyone outside the project management team. If questioned, team members were to instruct the requester to contact the programme manager directly for information. In this way, Judy's project communication management approach reflected the defined conventions and, at the same time, put procedures and mechanisms in place for dealing with highly confidential information within the project management team.

## Set up the project controls

| Description: |
| --- |
| *The level of control required by the project board after initiation needs to be agreed and the mechanism for such controls needs to be established – as does the level of control required by the project manager of the work to be undertaken by team managers.* |
| *Project controls enable the project to be managed in an effective manner that is consistent with the scale, risks, complexity and importance of the project. Effective* |

> *project controls are a prerequisite for managing by*
> *exception.*

### What this means

Now that you've decided how to do things during this project, make sure the mechanisms you've decided to use are in place and ready for use. For example, if you wanted to use a Microsoft Excel spreadsheet to capture issues and changes, you would need to make sure that the spreadsheet template was created and stored in the correct location, and appropriate access permissions were granted for those who would need to access it. Also, if decisions have been made on how to delegate responsibilities for risk, change control, quality and communication management throughout the project management team, then all the team members' role descriptions will need to be updated to reflect these decisions and new or amended authority levels.

### Illustration

In his communication management approach, Darren decided that he would set up a project email address. This way, if any stakeholder – internal or external – needed to reach the project management team, they could use this designated address. He even came up with a clever address: *project_help@project.com*. This was his answer to capturing feedback and allowing the project communications to be truly bidirectional. Not only would it be a great communication tool to push messages out to stakeholders and team members about the project, but it would also act as a receptacle for collecting feedback.

The project board was so impressed by Darren's forward-thinking and proactive approach to engaging stakeholders that they failed to see that he had forgotten to actually create the account. The email address was published repeatedly in project documentation, pamphlets, user guides and Internet and intranet sites. Yet, whenever anyone attempted to use it, their messages were bounced back to them as "undeliverable." This did not sit well with the stakeholders, who felt that the project team was purposefully and maliciously trying to ignore their feedback by publicising an e-mail address that didn't work!

The project board – who is responsible for the communications between the project management team and stakeholders external to that team – went into overdrive to repair relations. Measures were put in place to make sure this did not happen again. Not only was it logged in both the issue register and lesson log, but an immediate lessons report was distributed to the rest of the organisation detailing this significant mistake.

**Create the project plan**

---

### Description:

*Before committing to major expenditure on the project, the timescale and resource requirements must be established. This information is held in the project plan and is needed, so that the business case can be refined and the project board can control the project.*

*Planning is not an activity that the project manager performs in isolation but, rather, something that should be done with close involvement of the user(s) and supplier(s). It is often useful holding planning workshops to help identify all the products required, their details, and the dependencies between them.*

---

## *What this means*

Even though the plan will change, an estimate is needed to establish an overall sense of what time, money and resources will be required for the project. A high-level, overarching estimate will suffice in giving the project board a mental picture of how long this project will take, as well as how much money and how many resources will be used and when. Without this picture, the project board may have the false impression that the project will take a lot less time, and so may begin overbooking resources and over-promising results. Or (possibly worse), they may assume the project will take a lot longer and start shying away from such a taxing investment of time, money and people. The project plan will be broken into management stages, demonstrating the logical steps to get to the end result. The project board will be able to see the overall path, but will only need to commit to one management stage at a time. After each management stage, the project plan will be updated to show the latest thinking and the latest estimates on what it will take to complete the project.

## *Illustration*

When the new local government officials were elected into office, they had made some fairly lofty promises. Their main pledge – and the one that won them the election – was to upgrade and improve all the local schools to the best possible standards within the next five years.

The timeline was clear: five years. The objectives were clear: to improve and update all the local schools. The details of how this was to be done, however, were not. A project plan only needs to show the major, high-level products and activities of the project, so that the overall timeline, costs and achievability of the end goal(s) can be assessed.

From their first day in office, the new officials were working on the new project. They couldn't complete it all at once, so broke the effort into management stages. The School Upgrade Project (SUP) was launched to research, design, build, test, and rollout the new and/or improved schools to their community members, staff and students. The project plan showed a high level of the order of products (upgraded schools) and activities (designing, building and testing), but not the detail needed to actually achieve them. Additionally, it proved that the project could be done within the existing constraints of time, cost and quality, and provided an estimate for the timescale and resource requirements.

In order to complete the project plan, the project manager worked with community groups, students and staff members (the users), as well as architects, building contractors and building regulators (the suppliers). He facilitated multiple workshops and planning meetings to identify all the products and their dependency relationships.

In the end, it took a sixth year to complete the last few schools. Though their timelines were adjusted to address economic ups and downs along the way, they kept their promise and were consequently re-elected into office (another benefit for them).

**Refine the business case**

| Description: |
| --- |
| *The outline business case produced during starting up a project needs to be updated to reflect the estimated time and costs, as determined by the project plan, and the aggregated risks from the updated risk register.*<br><br>*The detailed business case will be used by the project board to authorise the project and provides the basis of the ongoing check that the project remains viable.* |

*What this means*

Towards the end of the initiation stage, a lot more will be known about a project than could have been known in the starting up a project process. At this point, details about the project – which can be backed up with research and investigation – can be added to the business case. Timescales and costs can be verified through the project plan. Benefits can be validated via the benefits management approach, and an overall risk profile can be substantiated in the risk register. If, after the detailed exploration and analysis performed in the initiating a project process, a convincing and compelling business case can still be produced, then the project has a good chance of continuing into the subsequent stages, where the specialist work can finally begin.

*Illustration*

Dina owned the business case for the project. She was the project board executive. However, she did not have sufficient time or availability to actually produce the business case. She delegated this task to Sienna, the project manager. Sienna was unfamiliar with the user community and their needs, their potential for change and their capacity to achieve benefits, so she relied on the senior user to help her identify and define the benefits for the project. Unfortunately, the senior user – in her enthusiasm, or over-enthusiasm – started to bite off more than she could chew. The benefits she was specifying were lofty at best, unrealistic at worst. With Dina (the executive) too busy to notice, no one checked or double-checked the validity of these benefits. The business case – the justification for doing the project – was over-reliant on shaky, somewhat questionable benefits.

As could have been expected, the project was completed on time and to budget, but did not deliver on more than half of the predicted benefits. Lessons were learned – especially by the executive – to dedicate time and effort to assuring that the responsibilities to check and double-check the validity of the benefits being predicted are taken either personally or by a dedicated resource. For the executive – as the owner of the overall set of benefits from the project – this was a costly lesson, and one that she would not repeat again.

**Assemble the project initiation documentation (PID)**

| Description: |
|---|
| *There needs to be a focal point at which all information relating the "what, why, who, how, where, when and how much" of the project is:* <br><br> • *Gathered for agreement by the key stakeholders* <br> • *Available for guidance and information for those involved in the project.* |

*This information is collated into the project initiation documentation. The project initiation documentation is an aggregation of many of the management products created during initiation and used to gain authorisation for the project to proceed. It is not necessarily (and rarely) a single document, but a collection of documents.*

### What this means

This step does not state that a PID must be created, written or documented precisely, because it has already been created, written and documented. The PID has already been completed, refined and built up throughout the starting up a project and initiating a project processes. At this point, it merely needs to be converted into a format that is usable by the project's board members. The format of the documentation – as an email, zipped, posted on an intranet site, or printed for a direct handover – will dictate how the assembly work will be conducted.

### Illustration

Georgina – the senior supplier – is visually impaired, so required the PID to be printed in large print and presented to her in a binder. Maxine – the executive – is blind, so required the PID to be printed in Braille in several bound volumes. Celina – the senior user – is also blind, but preferred her copy to be sent electronically and without any graphics, so that her screen reader software, JAWS®, could translate it to her out-loud. The plan for the initiation stage detailed the tasks and resources required to compile the PID to these specifications for the project board members. The project manager followed this plan to ensure the right copy in the right format was delivered to the right member.

## Tailoring guidelines

---

### Description:

*Just because PRINCE2 has separate management products in this process, it does not mean each management product is reflected in a discrete and separate document or even as a document at all, where information and collaborate systems are used.*

---

### *What this means*

Regardless of how this process is documented, the fact that the rest of the project will be built on the firm foundations set in this process is the key attribute of this process. Some projects will require substantial research and documentation whilst others can rely on discussions or workshops backed up with meeting minutes to evidence the exchanges, compromises and resolutions regarding the direction and management for the project.

### *Illustration of common situations*

- **Initiating a simple project**
  Sophia documented her PID in a single document based on her company's template for small projects. It was an informal form that combined the project initiation documentation into one single presentation, easy to read by her executive who would sign this to evidence her official decision to authorise the project.

- **Initiating projects using an agile delivery approach**
  As project manager, Nolan, helped lead his team through the process of defining prioritising user stories to document the project requirements. As the project was using an agile approach, and the focus of tolerance

was on scope, the user stories captured the business needs. This allowed the team to develop the solution iteratively in increments, instead of creating product descriptions up front. Nolan's high-level plan from this process also included several incremental releases throughout the project.

- **Initiating a project from a supplier perspective**
  Madelyn signed the contract legally binding her organisation to conduct the specialist work for the customer. This was done after diligent negotiations over scope, times, price and quality expectations between the two parties. The initiating a project process was concluded with this contract being formally agreed.

- **Initiating a project within a programme**
  Most of the decisions on how to manage the project were already chosen for Gavin. His project was part of a larger, overarching programme. The programme manager mandated that he use the programme's management strategies as a basis for his risk management, change control, and communication management approaches. The only area that didn't neatly fit within the programme strategies was quality. Many of the standards and procedures were unique and different for the specialist work to be done on his project. That being the case, the programme manager gave leeway to Gavin to define his approach for quality, but only if done in conjunction with the quality expert in the programme management office.

# CHAPTER 8: CONTROLLING A STAGE

## Work packages: Authorise a work package

| Description: |
| :--- |
| *If people who are working on the project were to start activities whenever they thought fit, it would be chaotic. There must be a level of autonomy with the project team(s), but there will be wider issues involved of which they cannot be expected to be aware. It is therefore important that work only commences and continues with the consent of the project manager. The vehicle for this is the production, execution and delivery of a work package.* |

*What this means*

For a project manager to remain in control of a management stage, they must know what is happening in that stage at all times. Using work packages, they can decide how and when to authorise work to begin, continue and end. It's not enough for the project manager to delegate work to team managers; a corresponding acceptance of the work package will also be required. In the negotiations of asking for work to be completed and the accepting of that work, the project manager and team manager will need to decide and agree on procedures, communications, planning efforts, quality activities, targets, tolerances and completion procedures. Hopefully, a lot – if not all – of this will have been discussed during the planning process for the management stage, where the team manager's involvement will have provided useful information and insight into the work being asked for in the work package.

## Illustration

Cheryl sent an email to Anne. Her email asked Anne to pull together some facts and figures Cheryl needed for a report she was writing. She was going to be working on the report remotely, and would be in the office on Thursday afternoon to pick up the data. After sending the email, Cheryl crossed this task off her list and continued working on her report. She took the train into the office on Thursday around noon, arriving just after one o'clock. When she got to the office, Anne was not at her desk. She looked around the office for Anne, and finally found her in the break-out area, chatting to some co-workers. The first thing she noticed was that Anne appeared very relaxed.

Anne confirmed Cheryl's fears: she had just gotten back from her holiday abroad late last night. She was really groggy today and was still working her way through the 300 emails waiting in her inbox.

Oops! Cheryl had forgotten the most important part of authorising a work package: the all-important obligatory response from the team manager, indicating their acceptance. Without this, the project manager does not know if the team manager has truly understood or, in this case, even received the work package. If the team manager hasn't accepted it, there is little to no hope that the work will be done at all, much less to the standards and constraints defined in the work package. In the future, Cheryl will now request an email or phone call acknowledging receipt of such emails.

## Work packages: Review work package status

| Description: |
|---|
| *This activity provides the means for a regular assessment of the status of the work package(s). The frequency and formality of this activity will usually be aligned with the frequency of reporting defined in the work package(s) and supported by the stage plan for the current management stage.* |

### What this means

During the execution of the work package, the team manager will report information regularly via checkpoint reports. It is the responsibility of the project manager to review these reports against what was hoped would happen (as set out either in the agreed work package or the team plan). The actual progress information will need to be added to the stage plan and checked against the quality register to assess if progress is being made at the desired speed and accuracy.

### Illustration

Jacqueline currently has ten team managers working on ten different pieces of work for her project. Today is Friday, so she is expecting ten checkpoint reports via email by the end of the day. Although her own highlight report is not due to the project board members until the end of the month, she has taken the decision to receive weekly reports from all the team managers. With ten different streams of work occurring at the same time, she needs to be able to stay on top of the work and spot any problem or weak areas to deal with them before they become real issues.

When she receives the progress information from her team managers, Jacqueline refers to her supporting documentation to see if there are any new or potential problems. She reviews the work package and/or team plan to determine if the progress made to date is equal to that which was predicted, and if the work is still expected to be completed on time and to budget. Additionally, she reviews the quality register to ensure consistency of information about the quality management activities to date.

Based on all this information from all ten of her team managers, Jacqueline will need to update her stage plan to reflect this current data and any new forecasts or adjustments. She may need to update the risk register and/or issue register, as well.

**Work packages: Receive completed work packages**

| Description: |
|---|
| *Where work has been allocated to individuals or teams, there should be a matching confirmation that the work has been completed and approved.* |
| *Once approved, any subsequent changes to the product(s) must pass through change control. This should be an automatic part of any change control method being used.* |

*What this means*

Just because a team manager claims to be finished with a piece of work does not necessarily mean they really are. The project manager must look to the quality register to confirm that the products allocated to the team manager have been tested and approved. Only after confirmation that the work has been completed can the project manager release the team manager from their obligations regarding this work package. If the two parties should meet again during this project, it will be because of a new and different work package, because – as it has been confirmed – this one has been completed.

### *Illustration*

John was very busy when the team manager phoned up to tell him that the product he'd been working on had been completed. John asked him if it had been tested. The team manager confirmed it had. John then agreed to take the product back and officially signed off on the work.

What John didn't know – and the team manager had forgotten – was that, although the product had been tested, there were a few minor errors that still needed correcting. The action items recorded in the quality check had been written on a scrap piece of paper that had become mixed up with and lost inside a large pile of other company documentation. This was then filed in a massive filing cabinet at headquarters three weeks later, never to be seen again.

When users started calling John to report problems with the product, John called the team manager. The team manager listened intently to what John was telling him about the problems and even agreed to help fix them, for a price!

The fact that John had signed off the product without checking the quality register to confirm the product had indeed been approved, meant that John now needed to re-hire the team manager to come back and fix the work. Realising that this might strain the relationship, the team manager agreed to do the work at a discounted rate, but still needed to charge the project, as this was a commercial agreement and the project manager was authorising a new work package. The old one had been officially and unequivocally received back.

**Monitoring and reporting: Review the management stage status**

---

### Description:

*If the project is not checked on a timely basis, there is a danger that it will get out of control. There needs to be a balance between planning ahead and reacting to events.*

*In order to make informed decisions and exercise rational control, it is necessary to compare what has actually happened with what was expected to happen and what might happen next (including issues and risks). It is, therefore, essential to have a steady flow of information that provides an overall view of progress and simple, robust monitoring systems to supply that information.*

*The objective of this activity, therefore, is to maintain an accurate and current picture of progress on the work being carried out and the status of resources. This activity occurs at a frequency defined in the stage plan, may be triggered by project board advice, or forms part of the analysis of new issues and risks.*

---

*What this means*

For a project manager to fully understand how the management stage that they are responsible for is performing, they need information. It is not just the ownership of information though; the information will need to be checked and analysed. In order for that information to be analysed, it needs to be collected. In order for it to be collected, a method of collection needs to be planned for.

The stage plan will set out regular activities for the project manager (possibly with the aid of project support) to pull together data about the stage. Data will need to be amassed from the checkpoint reports received from the team manager(s), new and amended issues and changes in the issue register, new and amended threats and opportunities in the risk register, and updated records in the quality register. All of the data will need to be collated, reviewed and scrutinised against the planned estimates. If, based on the inspection, the management stage is predicted to stay within its tolerances, then the next step will be to send a highlight report at the designated frequency required by the project board. If, however, the assessment predicts that the management stage cannot be completed within its tolerances, then the next step will be to issue an exception report immediately.

### *Illustration*

With the help of project support, Jayne set up arrangements to directly receive all the checkpoint reports from the team managers. Having gained these, she would then transfer the relevant data from the reports to the stage plan, issue register and risk register. Project support staff were also to be the first ones to be notified when a product had been completed, tested and approved, so that they could update the configuration item records to keep them in line with the updated quality register. Then, as project manager, Jayne would review the updated documentation every Tuesday to evaluate the stage status. This review often prompted her to perform one or more actions – such as taking corrective action or authorising a new work package – or triggered her to move into the managing a stage boundary process, if she was approaching the end of the management stage.

**Monitoring and reporting: Report highlights**

| Description: |
|---|
| *The project manager must provide the project board with summary information about the status of the management stage and project and distribute other information to stakeholders at a frequency documented in the communication management approach.* |

*What this means*

During the project, the project board will be busy in management meetings and other senior management activities. They will have set the stage boundaries and delegated stage-level tolerances to the project manager. They know that, at the end of this management stage, they will be notified of the stage's completion and provided with a plan for the next stage. However, it may be a long time before the current management stage ends, and they will need confirmation and a reaffirming message from the project manager to tell them the stage is on track. A regular report (a highlight report) providing highlights of the work completed so far, the work to be done, and an update on issues, risks and quality will help the project board stay connected with the project, its status, and the justification for its continuation. Without this regular flow of information, the project board may feel disconnected and become dispassionate. The project will just fall off their radar. Highlight reports confirm to the project board that the project is being managed carefully and with skill by the project manager. They may also prompt one or more members of the project board to make use of the 'give ad hoc direction' activity, or ask questions or for clarification about the report. This will demonstrate their level of interest and involvement in the project effort.

### *Illustration*

Gillian was asked by the project board to use a corporate template to report the project highlights once a month. To capture the right information for the template, she modified it for her team managers to use for their checkpoint reports. Now, she was guaranteed to receive regular, consistent progress information updates that she could easily summarise and present to the project board in whichever format they requested.

### Issues and risks: Capture and examine issues and risks

| **Description:** |
|---|
| *In the course of managing the project, various issues will occur, and risks may be identified. They will arrive in an ad hoc manner and will need to be captured in a consistent and reliable way. Any member of the project, corporate, programme management or the customer, the project or other stakeholders may raise an issue or risk.* <br><br> *Before making a decision on a course of action, each issue or risk should be registered and then assessed for its impact.* |

### What this means

As a PRINCE2 practitioner – one who uses and practices PRINCE2 – the project manager should know that the difference between a risk and an issue concerns the level of certainty surrounding it. A risk is a future uncertain event or set of events that may or may not happen, whereas an issue is a certain event that has occurred or will happen. Stakeholders in and around the project team may or may not also know this distinction. Many might be under the common false impression that risks are always in the future and issues are always in the past. So, when these stakeholders with different interpretations call on the project manager with a problem, issue, concern, query, threat or opportunity, they may or may not be using the correct terminology to describe what they mean. Regardless of their use of these terms, the project manager needs a mechanism for capturing these comments and analysing them with a consistent approach.

There are different procedures for both. The risk management procedures are documented in the risk management approach and the change and issues procedures are documented in the change control approach. The project manager will use the project's risk register and issue register to manage risks and issues as they are raised. The guidance in the approaches will help the project manager to assess the risks and issues correctly and either manage them within their limits or escalate appropriately.

### Illustration

Matt created a database for the project. It was set up to capture both issues and risks. He web-enabled the database, so that anyone could log on and add new issues and risks from anywhere around the world. Because an issue or risk would already have been captured, he could then start from the point of examining and finish the processes from there. This freed up more time for him to spend managing the project, instead of doing administrative work. He decided that, weekly, he would review the database and perform issue and risk management activities. On paper, this looked like an efficient use of Matt's time and expertise. His project board agreed and authorised his plans.

After one week, Matt realised that the open access policy for the database was not working. Members of the public, hackers, and other miscreants were clogging up his database with useless rubbish. He reset the access limitations so only project management team members and identified project stakeholders could log on.

After two weeks, Matt realised that no one, besides himself, knew the difference between a risk and an issue. He reset the fields to capture the comments, and he then made the necessary distinction himself when managing them.

After three weeks, Matt realised that the peaks and troughs of the project activity were frequent and sporadic, making his once-a-week rule inadequate for managing the risks and issues. He increased his frequency to twice a week.

After four weeks, Matt found that he had struck the right balance for capturing issues and risks for his project. He updated his lessons log and reported on his findings in his next highlight report.

## Issues and risks: Escalate issues and risks

---

### Description:

*A management stage should not exceed the tolerances agreed with the project board. The project manager can only take corrective action or maintain the status quo as long as the management stage (or project) is forecast to be completed within the tolerances set by the project board. This activity applies where any corrective action with the project manager's control would not save the management stage (or project) from going beyond the tolerances agreed. This applies to all types of issue and risk (or aggregation of them) that cannot be resolved within the tolerances set by the project board.*

*As it may take some time to gather the information to create an exception report, it is recommended that the project board be alerted as early as possible. Therefore, the project manager may wish to execute this activity in two steps: an early notification to the project board of the forecast exception situation to prepare them, followed by supporting information in the form of an exception report.*

*Escalating issues and risks is good practice and should not be seen as failure. The earlier that issues are escalated, the more time is available to implement any corrective actions.*

---

### What this means

If a new risk or issue impacts the management stage such that its forecast now exceeds its tolerances, and there is nothing that the project manager can do to bring the stage-level tolerances back within their limits, the project manager no longer has the authority to make decisions regarding this management stage. An exception report must be escalated immediately to the project board. There is no grey area around this distinction between forecasting inside stage-level tolerances and outside them. As soon as the project manager recognises that they cannot keep the forecast for the management stage within its tolerances, they must escalate the situation. Attempting to hide or mask the problem will only make things worse. The sooner the project board members, with their authority and levels of seniority, are involved with exception situations, the faster they can help resolve them. The project board will approve how this should work via the controls originally set up in the initiating a project process – i.e. if they want verbal exception reports in person or on the phone or, if they want written ones, what format they are required in, etc. Additionally, if the exception situation pushes the project outside the project-level tolerances within which they operate, the project board will need to escalate it to the corporate, programme management or the customer above them.

### *Illustration*

Joleen's team manager raised an issue about a local flooding, which was causing a time delay for his work package. After assessing the issue and looking at her options, Joleen decided to make additional time tolerance available to the team manager. When a second delay occurred because of a strike in Eastern Europe, she used her cost tolerance to pay for additional resources to help catch up on lost time. By the third delay – this time resulting from an active volcano in Iceland – Joleen was out of time and cost stage-level tolerances. She looked at the product descriptions to determine if there were any quality tolerances that could be applied, which could potentially lessen the workload for the team manager to counteract the delay. There were none. None of the options she considered would bring all the stage-level tolerances inside their limits. She then immediately escalated the issue via an exception report to the project board. She included all the options to resolve the situation that she could think of, but was not able to authorise these herself. She indicated that her recommended option would be to increase the management stage's time tolerances, allowing Joleen to finish the stage within the new limits.

### Issues and risks: Take corrective action

---

**Description:**

*Changes and adjustments to the project need to be made in a considered and rational way, even when they appear to be easily manageable and within tolerances.*

*In taking corrective action, the objective is to select and, within the limits of the management stage and project tolerances, implement actions that will resolve deviations from the plan. Corrective action is triggered during the review of the management stage status and typically involves dealing with advice and guidance received from the project board, and with issues raised by team managers.*

---

*What this means*

If a new risk or issue does not cause the management stage to exceed its tolerances, or the project manager is able to keep all the stage-level tolerances within their limits, then they have the authority to make decisions regarding the desired solution. The litmus test is that all the stage-level tolerances remain within their set limits as directed by the project board. If this can be done, then the project manager can get on with the management stage and summarise the incident(s) and their resolutions in the next scheduled highlight report.

### *Illustration*

Marguerite bought her sons a Scalextric toy car racing track. Her eldest son worked out, over a brief period of trial and error experimentation, how to best manoeuvre around the tight corners and steep hills at just the right speeds and level of control in order to make it all the way around. The younger son kept losing control of his cars. He'd push them to go faster and faster until he lost control, spun off the track and was unable to complete the race.

The parallels to her work life were endless. The more work Marguerite tried to push through at breakneck speeds, the more problems and exceptions she ran into. Her boss was initially impressed with the speed Marguerite agreed to get things done. However, after the fifth exception situation in less than three weeks, he was becoming less and less impressed with her abilities. Marguerite reflected on this and decided to learn from her eldest son. By starting with a realistic plan then, over time, learning how to finesse the system and manoeuvre around obstacles, she would be able to stay in control – taking corrective action as she went, instead of escalating exceptions.

**Tailoring guidelines**

---

**Description:**

*The work packages are fundamentally important to this process as they relate to the PRINCE2 principle to focus on products.*

*The managing product delivery process is where specialist work is undertaken, work will be done using practices which are appropriate to the type of work. It is important that monitoring and control of specialist work is done using controls and measures which are appropriate to that work and that the project manager should incorporate them into the appropriate management products.*

---

*What this means*

The controlling a stage process should be as vigorous as necessary to stay in control of the specialist work conducted on the project. When multiple teams are working on multiple products, the specialist aspects of the project can quickly get out of control. The same can be said of projects where the project manager is also acting as the team manager. When focus is not on the right things - either managing or doing, things can quickly get out of control. This process puts into place the mechanisms required for the project manager to stay in control, no more and no less than what is needed. Demonstrating this appropriate level of control to the project board, project assurance and other key stakeholders is paramount to the confidence in the project and its management.

## *Illustration of common situations*

- **Controlling a stage on a simple project**
  Evan was working on a four-week project. He had the required specialist skills as well as experience of managing projects successfully. It was agreed that he would perform both project manager and team manager roles. He therefore did not keep a separate team plan, nor did he authorise himself written work packages. He simply managed his own time according to the role he was playing at the time. To demonstrate his progress and control over the work, he used a visible wall chart above his desk.

- **Controlling a stage when using an agile delivery approach**
  Kaylee is a developer on an agile project, her project manager has empowered her and the rest of the team to self-organise and plan the team's sprints, as they see fit. The project manager attends the daily stand-up meetings to observe, but allows the team, the experts to coordinate their own work. He is mainly there to deal with any issues or risks that arise. He gathers the progress information from their Kanban board and communicates that more widely to off-site stakeholders.

- **Controlling a stage from a supplier perspective**
  Salvador was the team manager on the customer's project team structure, but the project manager on his company's project team structure. He had a team of 15 staff who were working on the customer's project. To keep control over their work, he utilised the controlling a stage process to delegate the work via lower-level work packages and collected progress information that

he then summarised these into checkpoint report to the customer.

- **Controlling a stage of a project within a programme or portfolio**
  There were some differences for Maya because her project was part of a bigger programme. Her risk and issue registers were directly linked to her programme's risk and issue registers. The programme management office (PMO) provided expertise to analyse and respond to risks and issues. She also had to copy her programme manager and PMO when sending highlight reports to her project board. A few extra key performance indicators were being measured by the programme, so in her reports she had to include extra metrics that she'd not had to do before when working on stand-alone projects. And finally, she had to rigorously report on several external dependencies that were in place because of other projects within the programme. If any of these were late or had issues, she had a strict escalation route to follow to alert the programme manager immediately.

# CHAPTER 9: MANAGING PRODUCT DELIVERY

## Accept a work package

| Description: |
| --- |
| *The fundamental principle is that before a work package is allocated to a team, there should be agreement between the project manager and the team manager as to what is to be delivered, the reporting requirements, what constraints apply, any procedures to be applied, and whether the requirements of the work package are reasonable and can be achieved.* |

### *What this means*

This step figuratively or literally represents a handshake between the team manager and the project manager. The two parties must understand and agree to the work being requested and all the conditions of time, cost, quality, scope and effort.

The project manager is responsible for managing the project, not for doing the work. Therefore, they decide when work should be done, by whom and under what constraints. The team manager is paid to get the specialist work completed. When the project manager authorises a work package, the team manager agrees (most likely after some negotiation) to do the work within the specified timeframe and under the agreed constraints.

The project initiation documentation contains information about how the project is to be managed. In order to create the work package, the project manager pulls out the relevant information pertinent to the team manager and conveys these rules and constraints within the work package (for example, how risks are to be managed, how changes are to be captured, assessed and approved or rejected, and how quality is to be managed, monitored and controlled, etc.)

### *Illustration*

George, the project manager, signed a contract with a supplier to perform a piece of work. The supplier company did not use PRINCE2 to manage this piece of work, but that did not matter to George. What mattered to him was that the supplier agreed to the terms and conditions of the work package (in this case, the contract). The supplier agreed to make sure that the work would get done according to the contractual terms and conditions and that, when finished with the work, they would return it to George – again, according to the instructions agreed in the contract.

George's company had well-established working practices around the office. When incidents occurred, there were procedures for dealing with them. When communications were required, there were protocols that were followed. The company's document management system helped everyone comply with the organisation's version control requirements. So, when George authorised internal work packages, he did not need to write and agree a formal contract, as he did with the external supplier. Instead, he relied on their well-known and well-documented internal working procedures. Most of his internal work packages were in the form of emails. The team managers would then reply to the email to indicate their acceptance.

**Execute a work package**

| Description: |
|---|
| *The work has to be executed and monitored to the requirements defined in the authorised work package.*<br><br>*While developing the products, the team manager should not exceed the work package tolerances agreed with the project manager. The team manager can only proceed with the work package or take corrective action while the work package is forecast to complete with the tolerances set by the project manager. As soon as work package tolerances are forecast to be exceeded, the team managers should raise an issue to the project manager who will decide upon a course of action.* |

*What this means*

Once the team manager has agreed to (and perhaps negotiated) the constraints laid out in the work package, they get on with the work. If there are problems or issues, the team manager raises an issue, so the project manager can manage them or escalate them to someone who can. If there are questions or conflicts, the team manager raises an issue, so the project manager can find the right resources to answer or fix them. If there are risks, the team manager raises an issue, so the project manager can use risk management to mitigate against them. This leaves the team manager without distraction and without obstacles, so they can get on with the work and report progress, as agreed.

## Illustration

Valentina was not only a specialist in her field, but a stay-at-home mum as well. She had agreed to take on a part-time effort covering a two-week work package for a project. She also agreed to complete the work according to recognised industry standards. The time she reserved for working on the project was between 8pm and midnight, when her children were in bed. The terms of the work package did not stipulate that she had to work during certain hours – only that she worked four hours per day. She sent her daily checkpoint reports in at midnight, and was thus in compliance with her daily progress reporting requirements. As the expert, Valentina got on with her work, which was impeccable. She completed her work within the agreed work package tolerances, and all her products passed their quality checks with flying colours.

### Deliver a work package

| Description: |
| --- |
| *Just as the work package was accepted from the project manager, notification of its completion must be returned to the project manager.* |

## What this means

This step represents the second handshake between the team manager and project manager. This time, the two are agreeing that the work that was delegated to the team manager in the work package is, in fact, complete. The project manager will need to be notified; possibly, project assurance and project support will also need to be notified when the work is complete. How all of this is to be done is documented in the work package.

***Illustration***

Sammie finished the last of the 20 products delegated to him in the work package. The previous 19 were sent back to project support for safe storage immediately after they had completed their quality checks. This time, Sammie not only had to call project support to come and pick up the last approved product, but he had to reference the work package to find out how he was supposed to advise the project manager of its completion. The instructions lead him to phone a mobile number and leave a voicemail message. After that, he was then to send a back-up email to the project manager, confirming the voicemail message had been left. In his email, he had to carbon copy three other team managers, one project assurance member and the manager of the project support team. Finally, once the voicemail and the email messages had been sent, Sammie was supposed to turn his work badge in to the front desk at reception and sign the consent form for his hypnotic-trance-memory-removal therapy sessions, before being chauffeured to his first session.

**Tailoring guidelines**

---

**Description:**

*The activities in this process may be combined, split or run concurrently to suit the context, but care should be taken to ensure the integrity of the interface to the controlling a stage process.*

---

*Work packages are not necessarily small in scale. All the PRINCE2 principles are as applicable to a work package as to a project, requiring appropriate governance and control and often needing a team manager who is skilled in project management. For large work packages, a team manager may create a hierarchy of smaller work packages to allocate to the team members. In this case, the process for managing product delivery should be tailored to ensure the work in any lower-level work packages is controlled.*

### What this means

Work packages can range from a verbal request to a colleague to a written, legally binding contract with an external supplier. It all depends on who the team manager is, the history and relationship they have with the project manager and if the team manager is even a different person than the project manager. Because of these extreme variations, this process needs to be tailored and adjusted accordingly, team manager by team manager, work package by work package. There is no one size fits all for the project. Each work package will need careful consideration about how much formality is required and what types of controls need to be put in place to ensure quality work is provided.

### Illustration of common situations

- **Managing product delivery on a simple project**
  Xavier sat next to his project manager. His work and progress were self-evident as it could clearly be seen on a daily basis. Even so, he still though gave regular progress updates, verbally. If there were problems or

questions, he also did not hesitate to stop, turn his head and ask.

- **Managing product delivery when using an agile delivery approach**
  Liliana was the project manager and played the team manager role. She used her leadership skills to encourage the team to work collaboratively in an open, honest, transparent nature. Their daily stand-up meetings helped form the team culture and build trust between team members, as they reported progress to each other daily. The iterative nature of their work meant that they didn't take things personally, but learned from each iteration and their work improved. The frequent releases also meant their confidence and trust in each other grew as they proved how well they could work together as a tight-knit team.

- **Managing product delivery from a supplier perspective**
  Parker's work package arrived via Fed-Ex® and required a signature for receipt. This legally binding contract outlined the exact timeframes and pricing structures for the work involved. The product descriptions were in the form of a detailed requirements document and a clear escalation route for problems was mapped out. There was no confusion of who to contact and how, if there were to be any issues with the work.

- **Managing product delivery on a project within a programme**
  As one of the project's team managers on the project, Selena did not notice any differences from working on a project within a programme. That's because as a team manager, there is no interface to the programme. Any

required interfaces are managed through the project board and/or project manager. Selena, an expert in her field, just got on with her specialist work based on the work packaged she accepted.

# CHAPTER 10: MANAGING A STAGE BOUNDARY

## Plan the next management stage

| Description: |
|---|
| *The stage plan for the next management stage is produced near the end of the current management stage. Closure activities should be planned as part of the stage plan for the final management stage.* |
| *Planning is not an activity undertaken in isolation. The project manager will need to consult with the project board, project assurance, team managers and possibly other stakeholders in order to create a viable plan. The more people involved in planning the more robust the plan will be (as long as the right people are involved).* |

### What this means

No project manager can accurately predict the distant future. Issues, risks and changes all impact a project in an ad hoc fashion, causing need for adjustments, modifications and corrections to be made along the way. For this reason, the project is broken into management stages, and only the next management stage is planned in detail. The project manager (possibly with the aid of team managers, project support and guidance from project assurance) should be able to plan in detail for the next management stage with some level of certainty. This planning activity, however, must only happen as close to the start of that management stage as possible. If done too early, then too many variants will have changed before the management stage arrives; if done too late, there will be gaps of unproductive down time in the project, wasting time and resources.

## *Illustration*

Natasha had been working in the organisation for three years. She was accustomed to the company culture, its seasonal variations and its cyclical patterns. As a project support member, efficient in planning tools and techniques, she helped project managers set up and plan their projects. Even though she had assisted previous project managers in producing lessons reports about planning, she was still often asked to review draft plans to spot common errors.

The most common oversight she noticed was over-scheduling resources during summer months and at the end of the year. Most employees at the company took their annual leave at these times. On top of this, those still working during these peak times were already over-subscribed with activities to sustain the business as usual environment. The second biggest mistake was not involving key corporate functions in the quality checking of products. The human resources (HR), finance and procurement teams were always impacted by business changes, but rarely consulted about or involved in them. And the third common major error was to plan too far in advance.

The company had a history of being severely impacted by the slightest of economic changes. Stage plans that made predictions for more than three or four months in the future tended to hit exception situations. Beyond this three- to four-month planning horizon, estimates in a stage plan were guesstimates or flat-out guesses. Due to her experience and influence, Natasha helped many project managers within the company avoid these important planning errors.

**Update the project plan**

> ## Description:
>
> ***The project board uses the project plan throughout the project to measure progress.***
>
> ***The project plan is updated to incorporate actual progress from the management stage that is finishing, and to include forecast duration and costs from the exception or stage plan for the management stage about to begin.***
>
> ***Details of any revised costs or end dates are used when updating the business case.***

*What this means*

Once a management stage is completed, the actual information about that management stage can be documented in the project plan. If the management stage was originally predicted to take three months, but actually took three months and two weeks, then this will impact the whole project plan. In the original project plan, that next management stage should have already started. The project plan now must be updated to reflect it starting two weeks later, which may cause the entire project to finish late.

Once the next stage plan has been created, the new estimates for it can be documented in the project plan. These new and better projections have just been made in the previous step. The likelihood is that these new estimates are quite different from the original ones represented in the project plan – this due to experience, new information and lessons learned from the previous management stage. These adjustments and corrections will need to be added to the project plan to provide a better, more accurate view of the overall project.

## *Illustration*

Yoshi's original project plan predicted that, over the two-year timeline, each management stage would take exactly three months to complete. After the first subsequent management stage, he realised that three months was too ambitious. The first management stage had completed within its stage time tolerance of an additional three weeks; however, the original project plan was now out of date. Yoshi used the 'save as' function on his project plan file and created a second version. This one recorded the actual information from the first subsequent management stage and new estimates for upcoming management stages. To help create better, more accurate estimates for the plan, Yoshi consulted again with project assurance and the team managers who were going to be responsible for the work. Having already experienced one subsequent management stage, all were better able to contribute. Their estimates were more accurate, they made fewer assumptions, and they were able to identify and analyse risks more thoroughly. The second version of the project plan comprised management stages with lengths ranging from three to five months (these depending on the different natures of the work being planned for), and a new overall time line spanning two years and two months.

**Update the business case**

| Description: |
|---|
| *It is a PRINCE2 principle that projects have continued business justification.*<br><br>*The project board is ordinarily only authorised to continue while the project remains viable (that is the benefits will be realised within the cost, time, quality, scope and risk parameters set out in the currently agreed business case).*<br><br>*Projects, however, do not take place in a static environment. The environment external to the project changes, as do the nature and timing of the project's products. The business case needs to reflect these changes and must be reviewed and amended to keep it relevant to the project.*<br><br>*As the executive is responsible for the business case, the project manager should consult with the executive when reviewing and updating the business case in preparation for project board approval.* |

*What this means*

With changes to the project plan reflecting new and updated forecasts for the remainder of the project, the timescales and costs sections of the business case – at the very minimum – will need updating. Furthermore, the need for the project will need to be checked and scrutinised. If the driving force behind the project disappears or diminishes, then the justification for the project expenditure is bound to disappear or diminish. A true and accurate portrayal of the continued justification for the project needs to be reflected in the updated business case.

### *Illustration*

The project board has elected to pay for the correction of an exception in the current management stage by de-scoping the project. The money initially allocated to creating one of the project's products was diverted to fixing the exception situation. The project manager was requested to produce an exception plan for this option, as well as to update the project plan, update the business case and write an end-stage report.

The effect on the business case was that the costs of the project remained the same, but the expected benefits decreased. The product being de-scoped contributed to the benefit of increasing sales by 50%. Without this benefit, the business case looked less and less desirable. However, when the project manager updated the business case to reflect these changes, she noticed that although the benefits were less than originally predicted, they were still well within the benefits tolerance for the project.

### Report management stage end

| Description: |
| :---: |
| *The results of a management stage should be reported back to the project board, so that progress is clearly visible to the project management team.* |
| *The project manager gives a view on the continuing ability of the project to meet the project plan and business case, and assess the overall risk situation.* |

> **This activity should happen as close as possible to the actual end of a management stage.**

## What this means

As close to the end of the management stage as possible, the project manager needs to take stock, sum everything up, and give an account to the project board. As the person who knows the ins and outs of the project the best, the project manager needs to do a review and recap the previous management stage. The project board will have been receiving highlight reports periodically since the previous decision was made – during the directing a project process – to authorise a stage or exception plan. However, this latest report is not about the progress of one management stage, but is rather an overall assessment of the stage and a view of the project's continuing viability. As a measure to ensure objectivity, the project assurance team will review the end-stage report. Based on this report and the next stage plan, the project board will decide to continue their investment in this project or prematurely close it down.

## Illustration

Jeremy was working on a high-profile project in his company. Since he was using PRINCE2, at the end of his current subsequent management stage he sent an end-stage report to the project board. In it, he declared that he was officially finishing the current management stage and was ready to take on the next one.

He gave a recap of the history and performance of the current management stage. He provided an executive summary of the current state of the updated business case, offering information on the benefits that had been achieved to date and an assessment of the benefits still expected. He confirmed that the project was still on target to achieve its objectives, and that the current management stage was just now finishing within its agreed targets and tolerances. He summarised the quality work completed and the performance of the products. He analysed the current management stage progress and provided statistics to show he was working within his tolerances. He ran through the issues and risks he had faced and how he had dealt with them. He summed up the team's efforts and identified some lessons learned. He even explained how he intended to apply those lessons with reference to the next stage plan.

Before handing the end-stage report and the supporting documentation to the project board, Jeremy showed it to project assurance. Minor errors and grammatical mistakes were caught in this review. Jeremy then sent the amended versions to the project board. He asked them to approve his current work and authorise him to move on to the next management stage.

Meanwhile, Marley, another project manager at the same company, attempted to cut corners in his end-stage report. Relying on his own memory of the progress made, the performance of his team, the quality of the work conducted, and the lessons learned, Marley's account of the management stage was misleading and inaccurate. Immediately, project assurance picked up on the mismatch between the supporting documentation, previous highlight reports and basic common sense. When called on it, Marley realised what he had done. His earnest attempt to save time and effort by cutting corners could have been disastrous, reflecting poorly on him and his team. With a new perspective and diligence to observing the standards and processes the organisation had put in place with PRINCE2,

Marley re-worked the end-stage report to the agreed level of quality required for his project.

**Produce an exception plan**

| Description: |
| --- |
| *If a management stage or the project is forecast to deviate beyond its agreed tolerances, it no longer has the approval of the project board.* |
| *Exception plans are requested by the project board in response to an exception report. Although an exception plan will be produced prior to the planned management stage boundary, its approval by the project board marks a management stage boundary for the revised management stage.* |

*What this means*

When a project manager is alerted to an issue, the first action they need to take is to capture it. After assessing the issue and determining its impact on the current management stage and project tolerances, they must look for options to correct it. If the issue is beyond the authority levels of the project manager – as documented in their stage-level tolerances – they must escalate the issue via an exception report. Based on the report, the project board can choose to fix the problem, close the project, or request an exception plan to show in detail how the situation could be resolved.

If the project board asks for an exception plan, then the project manager should then use the managing a stage boundary process to create one. In the exception report, the project manager would have presented several options for handling the exception situation. Based on these recommendations, or possibly one that the project manager had not thought of, the project board will request that the project manager re-plan.

Just because the project board has asked the project manager to create the plan does not mean that the project manager is authorised to use it yet. Once produced, the project board will need both the new plan and other additional information – an updated project plan, updated business case and an end-stage report – to help determine if they should continue to invest in the project or prematurely close it down.

### *Illustration*

Planning takes a long time and a lot of effort. It usually entails several rounds of workshops with team managers and project support, as well as reviews with project assurance. Only once a feasible and workable plan has been created and agreed can it be considered ready to present to the project board. So, when Tina started working on the exception plan before hearing back on the project board's decision about the exception report, she was wasting her own time, as well as that of many valuable company resources. It turned out that the project board had not made their decision for two days because they were hotly debating the merits of continuing with the project against those of prematurely closing it down. In the end, it was decided to close it down. No longer was the project worthwhile for the organisation. Tina was directed to move into the closing a project process to close it down prematurely.

Later, when the invoices started showing up at her manager's cost centre, Tina had a tough time explaining why she had been conducting workshops using company resources she was not authorised to use. She had hired expensive meeting rooms, spent money on coffee and lunches, and pulled staff members away from their business as usual jobs to work on a plan that, in the end, was not needed. The project manager should only produce an exception plan when requested to do so by the project board. As the project board represents the link between the project and other stakeholders – including corporate, programme management or the customer, there may be other considerations to consider while they make their decision about the future of the management stage and/or project.

**Tailoring guidelines**

| Description: |
| :---: |
| *The activities in this process may be combined, split or run concurrently to suit the context, but care should be taken to ensure the integrity of the interfaces with the initiating a project, controlling a stage and directing a project processes.* |
| *Although this process is called managing a stage boundary, it also covers the preparation of an exception plan within a stage when tolerances are exceeded; the PRINCE2 process model may therefore be changed to separate these two functions into different processes.* |

### *What this means*

The formality of this process is completely dependent on the level of formality required by the project board to decide to continue with the project - using a stage plan or an exception plan, or to stop the project. The project manager is responsible for this process to gather the latest, up-to-date information, either doing the leg-work themself or delegating parts or all of it to others.

### *Illustration of common situations*

- **Managing stage boundaries on a simple project**
  At the end of the only delivery stage on Mateo's project, the process of closing a project was invoked, so he did need the activities for managing a stage boundary. They were available, if an exception plan was requested, but none ever was. So instead of writing an end stage report, he wrote an end project report to sum up the one and only delivery stage.

- **Managing stage boundaries when using an agile delivery approach**
  Jasmine's project had the foresight to coordinate several sprints to fit within the management stages. At the end of an incremental release from the sprints, when the new features were being released into the operational environment, there was a natural, albeit short break to perform managing a stage boundary process to assess ongoing viability, re-prioritise, if necessary the remaining requirements and features before beginning the next increment/management stage.

- **Managing stage boundaries on a project from a supplier perspective**
  As the technical expert who would be working on the customer's next stage, Luis helped in the planning efforts. As the customer's project manager created their stage plan, Luis created his team plan, ready to use once authorised to do so in the next stage. The customer's stage boundaries provided Luis' organisation opportunities for putting in place their own decision points, such as resource usage and ongoing viability checks.

- **Managing stage boundaries on a project within a programme**
  Lorelei noticed that her project board had requested stage boundaries at the same time the programme they were a part of were scheduling end of tranche reviews. When she asked her executive for the reasoning behind this request, she told her that if the programme manager was to decide to close the programme down early at one of these reviews, then that would have knock-on effects to their project. Specifically, it would no longer be funded to continue. Instead of taking that risk, it was wiser to ensure that the funding stream from the programme was in place before approving the next management stage.

# CHAPTER 11: CLOSING A PROJECT

## Prepare planned closure

| Description: |
| :---: |
| *Before closure of the project can be recommended, the project manager must ensure that the expected results have all been achieved and delivered.* |

### *What this means*

Before closing down and handing over, the project manager has to confirm that the deliverables of this project have been provided. The project plan needs to be updated with all the actual information presented against the plans to prove all the work agreed on for this project has been completed. Additionally, a report will prove that all the products from the project have been granted with 'approved' status. The report – known as a product status account – will demonstrate that the products have all been tested and approved to meet their agreed quality criteria. And finally, the project manager needs to prepare to disband the team and get ready to release the project resources acquired for this temporary effort (for example, office space, computers, infrastructure, e-mail addresses, websites/intranet sites, etc.)

### *Illustration*

Jose knew the end was fast approaching. His team had been working together for the last two years but, before they could disband, Jose needed their help to finish off the last remaining tasks. The team managers helped by providing a timely and complete work package and quality information to aid Jose in updating the project plan with all the actual information from the final management stage. Project support helped confirm that every product from the project was indicated as 'approved' on the product status account. Project assurance for the senior user worked with Jose to confirm that the acceptance criteria listed in the project product description had all been met. Once complete, Jose sought approval from the project board to give notice to their programme management team above them that his team could soon be released.

**Prepare premature closure**

| Description: |
|---|
| *In some situations, the project board may have instructed the project manager to close the project prematurely. In such circumstances, the project manager must ensure that work in progress is not simply abandoned, but that the project salvages anything of value created to date and checks that any gaps left by the cancellation of the project are raised to corporate, programme management or the customer.* |

*What this means*

Either at an end-stage assessment or via ad hoc direction, the project board can request a premature closure. The issue register will need to reflect this project board decision, as it is, "a relevant event that has happened, that was not planned, and requires management action." The issue will need to record the resolution as the board's decision to prematurely close down the project, as well as the effects on the project.

Before closing it down prematurely, the project manager must confirm that what was agreed to be delivered up to this point in the project has been delivered. The project plan needs to be updated with actual information up to this point. Additionally, a product status account will prove the products created to date have been granted 'approved' status, meaning they have been tested and approved to have met their agreed quality criteria. And finally, the project manager needs to prepare to disband the team and get ready for an early release of the project resources acquired to date (for example, office space, computers, infrastructure, email addresses, websites/intranet sites, etc.)

### *Illustration*

A local council ran out of funding halfway through a building project. The objective of the project was to temporarily move residents out of their current public housing arrangements, demolish their dwellings, and rebuild better, more modern ones in their place. The project funding dried up after the residents were re-housed, but before the demolition activities could commence. The project board had no money left for the project, so they prematurely closed it down.

Even though the project did not finish, there were still completed products from the project that needed to be accepted by the council. In this case, the empty housing estate needed to be accepted by the council. It was completed and tested, in that all the residents had been moved and the building had been cleared for demolition. Additionally, the project had already acquired the necessary planning permissions for the new buildings. If new funding was to be found later, the council would have in their possession products that could be used straight away to complete the remainder of the project. If they don't recognise these as acceptable products, then their next project or change initiative will incur needless additional costs to perform work that has already been completed and tested.

**Hand over products**

| Description: |
|:---:|
| *The project's products must be passed on to an operational and maintenance environment prior to the project being closed. This may happen as a single release at the end of the project, or the project approach may include phased delivery where products are handed over in a number of releases.* |
| *It is not a project activity to undertake benefit reviews post-project, only to plan for such benefits reviews to occur.* |

*What this means*

The person or people who will soon be taking ownership of the products created from this project need to be given the products. They will also need information about the products (for example, details of open issues and open risks, along with their planned/suggested mitigating activities). The management over the products in the business-as-usual environment will want to know that the products are acceptable, and so will require evidence of acceptance records. The management will also need to know about any pending next steps for the products they are about to take ownership of (for example, ideas for future upgrades, predicted timings for impending modifications, etc.)

Additionally, the benefits management approach will need to be reviewed and updated with any actual benefits that have been measured and realised to date. The remaining benefit reviews will be planned for post-project, but will not be conducted by the project team. This benefits management approach needs to be handed over to the senior user(s) and executive. The senior user(s) will be held to account for the benefits realisation after the project. Here, however, they will be working in their business as usual roles – rather than as project team members – as the team will soon be disbanding.

### *Illustration*

When Ashley purchased his brand-new house, he didn't expect the estate agent to just hand him the front door keys and walk away. He needed more than that. He wanted the floor plans showing where the gas and water mains were located. He wanted the deed proving his outright ownership and the exact measurements of his property lines. He wanted the paperwork describing his home owner association rules and guidelines. He wanted a copy of his insurance and mortgage agreements. He wanted the warrantees that accompanied all the new household appliances. He expected all these things and more, so that he could not only own his new house, but he could use it – live in it, decorate it, paint it, grow a garden around it and refurbish it, if needed.

**Evaluate the project**

---

### Description:

*Successful organisations learn from their experiences with projects. When evaluating the project, the objective is to assess how successful or unsuccessful the project has been. It may also be possible to improve the estimation for future projects by analysing the estimates and actual progress metrics for this project.*

---

### *What this means*

As all the documentation has been updated with the actuals from the final management stage, the project manager, in consultation with the project management team, can look back and review how the experience of the project was for them. An objective assessment about targets, milestones, changes, risk management, performance and quality can be made. As well as this, valuable lessons from this experience need to be captured and shared. The end project report – informed by the management products created, updated and controlled throughout the project – will provide the useful assessment of the project's end result compared with its original intentions depicted in the project initiation documentation. The lessons report – informed by the issue register, risk register and quality register – will summarise key learnings that will be useful for any future project within the organisation.

### *Illustration*

Emily and Richard returned from their holiday in Greece. Their goal was to visit at least three islands, as well as the mainland. They wanted to see the Acropolis and four or five museums or churches. Their tour operator had provided them with all the tickets they needed to accomplish their desired itinerary. So why did they not achieve all of this on their trip? A thorough review of the events helped them see the problems and learn some valuable lessons for their next European excursion.

Richard enjoyed touring around the city of Athens more than he had anticipated, and prolonged their stay there by one day. Their problems started when they realised their ferry tickets were only valid for the date they were booked. They had to purchase new ones to replace the old ones. When they reached their first island, the hotel had cancelled their reservation because they did not show up the night before, but their credit card had been charged in compliance with the hotel cancellation policy. The hotel had already booked their room to another guest and there were no more vacancies. In fact, there were no vacancies at any of the hotels on the island. Richard and Emily were then forced to purchase more ferry tickets to another nearby island to find accommodation for the night.

When the time came for them to move on and catch up with their original itinerary, they discovered that the ferries to this island were not as frequent as the others. No ferries were due into port for another three days, causing them to miss their scheduled appointments and hotel reservations. They had to divert all their energy and holiday budget into getting back to Athens for their return flights, or risk losing those as well and paying even more penalty fares to get home on time.

From their lessons learned on this travel experience, their new family motto was changed from "live for the moment" to "pay that bit extra for flexible travel arrangements!"

## Recommend project closure

| Description: |
|---|
| *After the project manager has confirmed that the project can be closed, a closure recommendation should be raised with the project board.* |

### What this means

The communication management approach will specify the stakeholders who will need to be informed of the pending project closure. The project manager will draft a notification (the closure notification) that, if approved by the project board, will be sent to the identified stakeholders, alerting them to the fact that the project is closing. All of the project's registers and logs can then be closed down and archived for future audits. The project management team will remain in place until the project board makes their final decision to authorise project closure.

### Illustration

Collin reviewed the project's communication management approach to confirm who needed what information about the closing of his project. Based on the approach, he drafted the following items: a press release for the media, formal notifications to the suppliers suspending their contracts, and an internal company newsletter article announcing the successful completion of the project. He forwarded these to the project board with the end project report. If they decided to authorise its closure, the project board could then send these announcements out accordingly.

## Tailoring guidelines

<table>
<tr><td align="center">Description:</td></tr>
<tr><td>

*The activities in this process may be combined, split or run concurrently to suit the context, but care should be taken to ensure the integrity of the interface to the directing a project and controlling a stage processes.*

*If the final stage(s) of the project includes initial operation of the outputs, the handover products activity may not be undertaken in the project's final management stage as part of closing the project, but may happen within a number of previous management stages. Closing the project would then only require confirmation that all the handovers have been completed.*

</td></tr>
</table>

### What this means

The formality of this process is completely dependent on the level of formality required by the project board when deciding whether to close down the project. The project manager is responsible for this process, either doing the leg-work themself or delegating parts or all of it to others. The amount of effort required during this process usually depends on if the operational handover was done throughout the project in a phased roll out or at the end.

### Illustration of common situations

- **Closing a simple project**
  Miles met with the project board to review the end results of his project. He presented the team's successes as well as their lessons learned. As he was the one to be maintaining the solution in his business as usual role,

he confirmed that he had all the required information and supporting documentation to do so. When the meeting was over, the project board circulated the meeting minutes to alert the stakeholders that the project was finished.

- **Closing a project when using an agile delivery approach**
  At the end of Nayeli's agile project, the process of closing a project had mostly been covered through other work. The solution had been rolled out incrementally through frequent releases. Regular retrospective meetings at the end of each spring with the team meant that lessons were captured and learned. A final retrospective meeting caught unfinished work, such as handing over the benefits management approach to the senior user to ensure these were performed at the appropriate times.

- **Closing a project from a supplier perspective**
  Although the project finished three weeks ago, Vincent and his team were not disbanded. As part of their supplier contract, they needed to remain available to the customer for any maintenance issues over the next six months. They could work on other projects as long as any issues from this one received top priority, if they were to occur. So far, no issues had arisen.

- **Closing a project within a programme**
  As part of closing a project, Celeste sent her benefit management approach, with information about when and how to measure benefits post-project, to the programme management office (PMO). As part of the programme, their responsibilities included monitoring and measuring benefits from the interrelated projects within the programme.

# CHAPTER 12: ADDITIONAL SUGGESTIONS AND PROCEDURES

**Business case theme: Relationships between outputs, outcomes and benefits**

| Description: |
| :---: |
| ***In PRINCE2:*** |
| • *A project's output is any of the project's specialist products that are handed over to the user (or users)* <br> • *An outcome is the result of the change derived from using the project's outputs* <br> • *A benefit is the measurable improvement resulting from an outcome that is perceived as an advantage by one or more stakeholders.* |

*What this means*

The project is responsible for creating products. These products are the outputs, which are handed over to the user community (or communities) for use in business-as-usual. Just because the users have access to or knowledge of an output does not guarantee that they will actually use it. The outcome is the consequence of using the output. A change in behaviour (i.e. the outcome) happens by using the new output, and becomes embedded in the organisation when it is stable and considered the norm. The benefit(s) are the measurable improvements caused by this change in behaviour and new way of working.

### *Illustration*

Sarah's boss purchased licenses for Microsoft Outlook (the output). He wanted everyone on the team to start using Microsoft Outlook to keep track of appointments and schedules (a change in behaviour, i.e. the outcome). The benefits he wanted were for the company to be greener – killing less trees – and to be friendly – with everyone being transparent with their activities and schedules. Sarah, however, had an unusual attachment to her paper diary. Her life-long obsession with hand-writing out her daily schedule and being able to physically cross off items when completed gave her enormous satisfaction. She had yet to come across an electronic gadget or system that gave her the same level of pleasure. She had tried Microsoft Outlook before at her previous company, and found she was not able to stick with it.

When the order came from the boss himself, she really did give it a good try. At first, she tried entering her schedule into both the system and her paper diary, but that ended up taking too much time away from her actual work. She then only added meetings into Microsoft Outlook because she could not be disturbed during meetings; other activities she felt didn't warrant such protection from interruptions. So, for a while, her colleagues were aware when she was in a meeting and was not to be disturbed, but they were not aware of how else she spent her time. Those activities still went in her paper diary. Eventually, even the meetings stopped being recorded in Microsoft Outlook. No one knew what Sarah was doing, except for her administrative assistant, who had to keep ordering paper diaries for her.

Because Sarah was not using Microsoft Outlook, her behaviour did not change. She continued to be ultra-private and eco-unfriendly. As a senior manager not partaking in the behavioural change, she set a poor example to others in the organisation, who also preferred to keep privately held schedules (possibly not for the same reasons as Sarah). Thus, their behaviour did not change either.

A definite divide started growing within the company, with those who complied with the Microsoft Outlook diary rule on one side, and those that did not on the other. The outcasts who didn't use Microsoft Outlook were seen as secretive, manipulative and politically ruthless. Not only did they not want to save the world by contributing to a greener workplace, they were contributing to a conflict-ridden work environment. None of the benefits of using Microsoft Outlook were being realised; in fact, the opposite was occurring.

**Organisation theme: Stakeholder engagement**

| Description: |
|---|
| *Stakeholder engagement is the process of identifying and communicating effectively with those people or groups who have an interest in or influence on the project's outcome. It is usually carried out at the programme level. All projects need to have some level of some stakeholder engagement, particularly if not part of a programme.* |
| *Parties external to the project management team can exert a powerful influence on a project. Effective communication with key stakeholders, both internal and external to the corporate organisation, is essential to the project's success.* |

### What this means

The one rule with stakeholders is that you can't ignore them. If people feel ignored, they tend to get angry, disenchanted and despondent. If they hadn't been ignored, they could have been a true champion and advocate for your change efforts, but, after feeling slighted, it is unlikely they will support you (at least not until a lot of reparations have been made).

The one truism about stakeholders – which is sometimes the bane of the project manager's existence – is that you cannot choose them. The project management team members are chosen based on their skill, interest and availability. Project stakeholders exist whether you want them to or not.

To engage with stakeholders, their needs and interests need to be understood and a strategy put in place to either encourage their ongoing support, redirect their opposition into support or, at the very least, minimise the destructive and disruptive powers of their opposition.

### Illustration

A junior project manager working on his first ever project was responsible for implementing a new car park on derelict land inside a suburban neighbourhood. He did a fantastic job organising the external suppliers clearing the land, resurfacing the land, painting parking spaces with the maximum use of space, etc. The one thing he didn't do – and didn't even occur to him to do – was to engage with stakeholders.

Property owners in and around the neighbourhood saw the building work going on, but did not understand what it was or how it would impact them. Members of the local neighbourhood association started joining forces, riling public opinion against the new site. On the day the car park opened for business, there were the local residents standing in front of the entrance, linked arm in arm, not allowing anyone to park there.

If only the project manager had bothered to engage with these stakeholders sooner. Then, they would have understood that the money generated from the paid parking would be reinvested back into their neighbourhood. The lot would be manned 24/7 by security guards, who would deal with any riffraff traipsing through their community streets. And finally, parking would be restricted to 7am to 7pm, so no additional traffic would congest their streets at unsociable times of the night. All their concerns could have been addressed. Instead, pictures of their protest were plastered all over the front covers of the local newspapers.

**Quality theme: Recommended quality review technique**

| **Description:** |
| --- |
| *A quality inspection is a systematic, structured assessment of a product conducted in a planned, documented and organised fashion. There are a variety of systematic inspection techniques. In the absence of any other approach, PRINCE2 recommends the quality review technique, which complements the use of a product descriptions.* |

---

**Four review team roles:**

- **Chair – responsible for the overall conduct of the review**
  - **Presenter – introduces the product for review, represents the producer(s) of the product and coordinates and tracks work after the review**
    - **Reviewer – reviews the product**
- **Administrator – provides administrative support for the chair and records the results and actions.**

---

### What this means

*Step one: Preparing for the review*

Preparation entails taking care of the administration side of the review, checking that the product is ready to be reviewed, and distributing copies of the product to all the designated reviewers. It is important to note that, in this first step, the quality reviewers will review the product against the quality criteria described in its product description. If the product matches the quality criteria, or is within the defined quality tolerances, then the second and third steps may be achieved quite quickly.

If there are minor errors, such as spelling mistakes or misused punctuation, these can be marked up or annotated on the copy and returned to the presenter. However, if there are questions, concerns or comments about the product matching its criteria, then the reviewers are required to capture these on a question list, which will form the basis for the agenda for the second step: the review meeting.

*Step two: Suggested review meeting agenda*

The review chairperson who will be conducting the review meeting will be responsible for compiling and circulating a review meeting agenda to drive the discussions and to ensure the group stays on topic. The meeting, which an administrator will write minutes of, should discuss the product under review with the product's presenter, who will attempt to answer questions and clarify concerns. Together, the reviews will need to discuss and agree the review results: either 'complete,' 'conditionally complete' or 'incomplete'. If possible, and if the person/group with approval authority is present, the product could potentially be signed off in the meeting. Regardless of the result, the chair will close the review and inform interested parties of the review outcome.

*Step three: Review follow-up*

If agreed actions had been identified in the review meeting, then the presenter could coordinate them after the review meeting. Each action will require a follow-up – as agreed by the reviewers in the meeting – to ensure they have been completed. Once all the actions have been completed, the product can be signed off by the chair as 'complete'. The administrator can then provide the review outcome information to the appropriate parties and update the quality records.

### *Illustration*

*One: Preparing for the review from the presenter's perspective*

The recommendation paper that Nancy was working on was finally complete, just in time for the quality inspection that was scheduled for that week. Sylvia, the chair, called that morning to check she was ready. Because Nancy was the only producer of the product, she was in a good position to be the presenter as well. Sylvia also confirmed that all ten of the reviewers were all set and ready for the review. Nancy sent copies of her paper to the reviewers.

*Two: Suggested review meeting agenda from the chair's perspective*

Using the meeting agenda as a guide to focus the meeting, Sylvia opened the meeting by thanking everyone for taking time out from their busy schedules to attend the meeting. Since most of the ten reviewers came from different areas of the organisation and did not know each other, Sylvia asked everyone to introduce themselves and explain how this recommendation paper impacted their business area. From previous experiences, Sylvia knew that facilitating a group of strangers through an in-depth discussion would be difficult without them first understanding each other's perspectives.

Next, Sylvia asked Nancy to give a brief introduction to the paper, its background and purpose. After this, the group went through a product walkthrough. Nancy did a brilliant job walking the group through page by page, addressing the questions raised on the consolidated question list. Sylvia had sent her the consolidated list prior to the meeting, so Nancy would be prepared. And she was! She answered all their questions, and any items that required further actions were agreed by the reviewers and captured by Lillian, the administrator.

A few themes arose from the questions and agreed actions, so Sylvia led a group discussion to raise any other global or major questions. Each of these was then reviewed and actioned, all of which were also captured by Lillian.

The meeting lasted two hours and ended with the group reviewing all the action items, along with their responsibilities. The review result was 'conditionally complete'. Once the agreed actions had been fulfilled, the recommendation paper would be considered 'fit for purpose'.

*Three: Suggested review meeting agenda from the administrator perspective*

After the review meeting, Lillian still had a lot of work to do. She ensured that Nancy had the list actions, so she could coordinate them, as agreed in the meeting. She followed up with the reviewers that had responsibilities to sign off individual actions – as agreed in the meeting – so that the quality records could be maintained accurately.

She let Sylvia know when all the actions were complete, so, as chair, she could sign off that the recommendation paper was now complete. She then let Nancy know, so she could start the process of getting the product approved. Finally, before filing away all the quality records from the review, Lillian communicated the review outcome to the ten business areas that required the update.

## Plans theme: PRINCE2 recommended approach to product-based planning

| Description: |
| --- |
| *In the absence of any other approach, PRINCE2 recommends this approach to planning:*<br><br>*1. Design*ing *the plan*<br>*2. Defin*ing *and analy*sing *the products*<br>*3. Identify*ing *activities and dependencies*<br>*4. Prepar*ing *estimates*<br>*5. Prepar*ing a *schedule*<br>*6. Analy*sing *risks* to a plan<br>*7. Document*ing a *plan.* |

### *What this means*

*Step one: Designing the plan*

Of the seven steps for planning, the first one only needs to be done once, as a prerequisite to the rest of the steps. Once the format, presentation, planning tool and estimating method have all been chosen, then the rest of the planning activities can commence and be repeated, as necessary. PRINCE2 focuses on planning from a management perspective, to keep control over the project. Thus, decisions need to be made in this step regarding the number and length of management stages that will be acceptable for the project board and allow the project manager to remain in control over the delivery work on a stage-by-stage basis.

*Step two: Defining and analysing the products*

The first repeatable step of the planning process is to define and analyse products for the plan (*see Plans theme:*

*Product-based planning for more information*). This step ensures that the plan will be created with the intent of creating products, and that these products will be within the agreed scope of the plan. Defining the products involves agreeing the overall project scope and acceptance levels, whilst breaking down the components that make up the scope and agreeing their individual quality criteria on an individual basis. The product analysis confirms that the decomposition of products did not unintentionally add to scope and that there is a realistic path to achieving the entire subset products based on their logical sequence and dependencies.

## Step three: Identifying activities and dependencies

Once the products have been defined and analysed, the project manager (ideally with the assistance of project support and team managers) will begin to identify the activities required to create the products. If an activity is identified that has nothing to do with the creation, modification, acquisition, confirmation or approval of the plan's products, then the activity should be re-examined to ensure that it is really needed for the plan. Project resources are usually quite expensive – if not in money, then in time and opportunity costs – and so doing an activity 'just because' comes at a great expense to the project and the organisation.

## Step four: Preparing estimates

Based on the estimation method chosen in the planning prerequisite, time and cost estimations will need to be made for the activities. It is important to use the estimating method identified earlier. If it is successful for this plan, the lesson learned can be to repeat its use for future plans. If it is unsuccessful, it may need to be changed or modified accordingly for future plans.

## Step five: Preparing a schedule

The product flow diagram from product-based planning will be an excellent starting point for preparing the schedule. It shows the logical order of the creation of the plan's products. However, a lot of new information will now be known about the activities required for the plan – for example their estimated durations and costs, and resources availability. Some, if not all, of the flow will be modified to fit within these constraints when preparing the schedule.

## Step six: Analysing risks to a plan

Running alongside steps two to five is the step to analyse the risks. This exists because of the frequent identification of risks during the planning process. At each step, more information will be known about the plan and, therefore, more information will be known about what can go wrong (or right) with it. For each risk identified, a new item will need to be added to the risk register, and the chosen mitigating activities will need to be added to the plan.

## Step seven: Documenting a plan

Once the plan has gone through its iterative cycle enough times to ensure there are no more risks to be identified or managed and all the products and estimated activities have been scheduled, then the plan can be completed. A final written narrative can be added to describe the plan and the thinking that went into its creation (for example, explanations of the constraints, external dependencies, assumptions, monitoring and control requirements, and any risks mitigation activities).

### *Illustration*

Elizabeth decided to bake her first ever cake from scratch. She decided to use pen and paper to keep track of all the different aspects of baking; since she was so new to it, she didn't think she could keep it all straight in her head. The estimation method she chose to use was to double the preparation times recommended in her cookbook, but use the exact baking times.

She started her planning by defining the products – in this case, the ingredients she needed. She noted if she had the products already (external products) or if she would need to buy new ones (internal products). External products are ones that are required for the project, but they either already exist or are being created by someone else, such as another project. Internal products are ones that this project is responsible for creating, obtaining or modifying. Once Elizabeth had understood all the ingredients required, she identified the activities. She determined that she would need to buy the ingredients, mix them, and bake. The dependencies for these activities were that they must be done in that order. She estimated each activity using her estimation method, then scheduled them, so that the cake would be ready in time for dessert that evening. She ensured all her resources (the pans, oven and cooling tray) were going to be ready and available at the times she needed them.

As she reviewed the schedule, she built in a few fall-back plans, in case things didn't go according to plan. If, by the time the cake was due to go in the oven, she was running more than 10 minutes late, she would call the bakery down the road and order a take-away dessert instead.

Finally, Elizabeth documented her plan. She consolidated all her notes and ideas into a clear, concise narrative, reminding herself of her own planning assumptions (that she would not be interrupted, for example), her monitoring and control requirements (the use of the kitchen timer bell set at key milestones, for example), and her key risks and their responses (if running late, she would order in, for example).

**Plans theme: Product-based planning**

| Description: |
|---|
| *PRINCE2 recommends but does not mandate, the following approach to product-based planning:* <br><br> • *Writing a **project product description*** <br> • *Creating a **product breakdown structure*** <br> • *Writing **product descriptions*** <br> • *Creating **product flow diagram.*** |

*What this means*

*Step one: Writing a project product description*

Through discussions with the senior user and executive, the project manager must capture the customer's quality expectations and help them to define these in terms of measurable acceptance criteria. These measurable acceptance criteria will form the basis for the eventual sign-off and acceptance of the project at its completion. This description will only be required for the project plan. It may be updated at various points throughout the project – when requested by the project board via ad hoc direction – using the project's formal change control procedures.

**Illustration:** The project is to make a cheese sandwich for lunch. The expectations are that it is delicious, large enough to be satisfying, and fresh enough to be desirable. The measurable acceptance criteria include that it is made on the day it is served and has white bread and Swiss cheese (*to be continued*).

*Step two: Creating a product breakdown structure*

Next, the project is broken down into its major products for the project plan. For stage and/or team plans, the major products may be broken down even further to suit the level of plan required. Breaking down a product means identifying two or more sub-products or component pieces that make up the product. This can be done continually until the minutest component has been identified. However, if not required – due to the size and nature of the project and/or the plan – then it is not recommended to go into more detail.

**Illustration (*continued*):** The product breakdown structure should include the component parts of the cheese sandwich for lunch:

- Two slices of white bread
- Two slices of Swiss cheese
- Two slices of tomato
- One leaf of lettuce
- One pat of butter
- One pinch of salt

- External product: serving plate (external because another project is responsible for choosing the lunchtime tableware, and this project must use what they decide – it is external to our control).

(*to be continued*)

## Step three: Writing product descriptions

Once a product has been identified as required for the plan, a product description for that product needs to be created. Many of the products will not be created during the first (few) management stages. Neither the project manager nor the team manager will be able to remember the details of the product if they are not captured in a formal product description.

A good test to see if all the required products have been identified is to compare the project product description with the sum total of the product descriptions. They should be equal, with nothing new added and nothing originally intended forgotten.

**Illustration (*continued*):** For each of the products identified, product descriptions should define their minimum quality criteria and any allowable tolerances. For example, is there any tolerance around the choice that the cheese must be Swiss cheese? Will English mature cheddar suffice? Do the two slices of white bread have to be of a particular kind? Can it be white focaccia flat bread? Or white pitta bread? (*to be continued*)

## Step four: Creating a product flow diagram

One final step of product-based planning involves identifying the logical order of creation for the plan's products. In a one-directional flow, the products are sequenced in the order in which they should be created. For example, a draft product must precede the final version. This allows the planners to identify areas of risks where dependencies exist, especially from external sources.

**Illustration (*continued*):** The flow diagram will help determine if there are any dependencies in the creation or production of the products. For this example, all the sandwich products can be created, obtained or modified in any order – even concurrently. When multiple products can be created concurrently, this may indicate that the project work can be divided amongst several team members, who can work on separate pieces/products at the same time. This valuable information will come in handy during the scheduling step of the planning process. Alternatively, if a project's products have very strict linear production dependencies – i.e. each product cannot be started until the previous one has been completed – then, regardless of the number of resources thrown at this project effort, it will have negligible impact on the speed to completion.

**Risk theme: The risk management procedure**

---

### Description:

*PRINCE2 recommends, but does not mandate, a risk management procedure based on Management of Risk: Guidance for Practitioners (Office of Government Commerce, 2010):*

- *Identify (context and risks)*
- *Assess (estimate and evaluate)*
- *Plan*

---

- ***Implement***
- ***Communicate.***

All the steps are repeatable. When additional information becomes available, it is often necessary to repeat earlier steps based on the new information.

### *What this means*

*Step one: Identify (context)*

It is important to understand the project's objectives and its risk management approach for dealing with risks threatening those objectives. This contextual information will help with understanding how and why certain risks warrant extreme risk responses, and why others do not.

*Step two: Identify (risks)*

After understanding the project's context, it is easier to start identifying the project's risk. These are initially captured in the daily log during the starting up a project process, and are then moved to the risk register from the initiating a project process onwards throughout the project. The best way to capture individual risks is to state them in a cause-event-effect arrangement. The cause of a risk is the known element, the event resulting from the cause is the uncertain element, and the effect summarises the "so what?" element that indicates why this risk is even being considered for management.

*Step three: Assess (estimate)*

Every risk identified and captured in the risk register needs to be assessed by providing estimates for its impact, probability and proximity. The guidelines and scales for producing these estimates will be defined in the risk management approach. Simple scales for impact and probability might offer 'high', 'medium' and 'low' scores, with definitions or criteria for each. Proximity might be measured as 'near-term', 'mid-term' or 'long-term', with explanations for each.

### Step four: Assess (evaluate)

Understanding how big one risk is to the project is important, but equally important is an understanding of what the overall risk profile of the project is. By adding up all the threats and opportunities identified, a useful summary of the project's risks can be established. This is important for the project board when they are making decisions about the project. If the project becomes too risky, they may wish to prematurely close it down.

### Step five: Plan

After assessing the risk for its size of impact, probability and proximity, response activities need to be identified to manage the risk. Or, alternatively, a measured decision not to manage (and accept) the risk needs to be made and recorded for future reference. The response activity will need to be proportional to the probability and impact of the risk. The proactive actions will need to be included in the plans. Separate fall-back plans may need to be created and resourced for any reactionary activities chosen to mitigate the risk.

### Step six: Implement

Once the risk response has been chosen and included in the plans, it is the responsibility of the risk owner to manage the risk and it's identified response activities. If the risk owner is too busy to fulfil these activities, they may delegate the tasks to the risk actionee.

*Step seven: Communicate*

Throughout the entire risk management procedure, there needs to be constant, bi-directional flow of communication. The project management team needs to feel secure and confident in raising risks without recourse from political powers, blame or punishment. Reporting on risks needs to be open and transparent throughout the project, at all levels.

***Illustration***

Every autumn, Manjit faces the same threat on her journey to work. Because there will be leaves falling on the train tracks (the cause), the trains may be late (the uncertain event), and Manjit may be late to work (the effect). She has already begun informally managing this risk by mentally noting this problem at the end of the summer (identify). She assesses the risk by looking at the probability, impact and proximity. Because the train operator has put up a poster in her train station this autumn, warning passengers of possible delays due to leaves on the tracks, Manjit decides that the probability is high this year. The impact of being late to work is also high; she has been late before and is already on a written warning for punctuality. The proximity is near-term and constant throughout the autumn.

Because this risk is a threat, Manjit has six options. To avoid the threat, she could choose an alternative mode of transportation to work, such as driving her car or riding her bike. That way, any train delays would not impact her journey to work. She could reduce the risk by getting up earlier and taking an earlier train. Even if the earlier train was to be delayed, chances are it wouldn't be so delayed that she would be late to work. She could get up at the normal time and attempt to take her normal train – hoping it wouldn't be delayed – but have a fall-back plan in place to take a taxi to work if it was. She would need to ensure she always had enough cash on her every morning, in case she needed to call a taxi. No taxi driver would take her to work for free. There is no way for Manjit to transfer or share this risk, as the train operator is not prepared to accept any responsibility for delays due to leaves. Their placement of the poster in the station communicates this unwillingness loud and clear. And finally, Manjit could accept it, choosing to do nothing about the risk and continue to monitor it. If only she wasn't on a written warning already, she might be tempted to accept it. However, she elects to trial the reduction option first and then use her fall-back plan only if needed. By taking this course of action, she has allocated ownership of this risk to herself (she is the risk owner) and retained responsibility for the actions (she is also the risk actionee).

**Change theme: Issue and change control procedure**

**Description:**

***PRINCE2 provides a common approach to dealing with
requests for change, off-specifications and
problems/concerns:***

- ***Capture***
- ***Assess***
- ***Propose***
- ***Decide***
- ***Implement.***

*What this means*

*Step one: Capture*

Anyone can raise an issue. The exact procedure for how it
should be done should be documented in the change control
approach under the "issues and change control procedures"
section. However, not everyone involved or interested in
the project will know, or even have access to, these
documented procedures. Their first impulse should be to
contact the project manager. The project manager will have
documented the change control approach and will,
therefore, know its contents intimately. They can then take
down the issue in the manner and format defined in the
approach. Because of the administrative nature of this task,
the project manager may have delegated some or all of this
step to project support.

*Step two: Assess*

Once captured, a full and proper examination of the issue must be conducted. The assessment should consider the impact of the issue on the achievement of the project's objectives, as well as the impact on the six areas of tolerance within the project manager's control: time, cost, quality, scope, benefits and risks. An assessment of the impact against the overall project tolerances should also be carried out.

*Step three: Propose*

The project manager should investigate several options for dealing with the issue, including the option to do nothing. If they have the authority to act over the issue, then the project manager can move on to the next step. If the issue pulls the project manager outside of their stage-level tolerances, then they must escalate the issue via an exception report first.

*Step four: Decide*

Once the issue or exception has reached the right level of management (the person or group who has authority to decide on the corrective action), they can make a decision about it. Their decision must be recorded and cross-referenced in the issue report and/or issue register. Any corrective action should be reflected in the appropriate plan(s).

*Step five: Implement*

Based on the decision made about the issue or exception, the project manager should implement the actions and include them in the plans. The results of these actions may also need to be updated in the issue report and/or issue register.

## *Illustration*

A user called the IT office and reached an IT team member working on the new system that had just been rolled out into the user's department. The user requested that a certain field on the user interface screen be moved from the left-hand side to the right. The team member saw it as a minor cosmetic request. He happened to have that file open at the time of the phone call, so he agreed there and then to change it for the user.

At around 3am that night, as the new system was going through its normally scheduled batch processing, it started to fail. Because of the failure, senior managers around the country were receiving text messages to call into an emergency conference call. As it turned out, 13 related systems that were searching for information from the field which had moved were programmed to look for it in a certain location. When it was moved, they could no longer locate the information and were no longer able to communicate or continue with the batch processing. A lot of angry and tired managers on the conference call were demanding heads roll.

Never in a million years should the IT team member have taken such a change decision without following a formal change control process. Even if they had the authority to make decisions about requests for change, an assessment of the impact from that change would have immediately shown that it was not a cosmetic alteration, but rather an intricate and complicated modification.

The same concept applies to projects. When undetected, undocumented changes that occur on projects are no longer operating in a controlled environment. When users want to add seemingly minor additions, when suppliers want to remove seemingly duplicate products, and when new legislation requires seemingly small adjustments for compliance, the project manager's knee-jerk reaction should be to pull out the issue log and start capturing.

**Progress theme: Types of control**

| Description: |
|---|
| *PRINCE2 provides two types of progress control throughout the life of a project:* |
| *Event-driven controls - These take place when a specific event occurs.* |
| *Time-driven controls - These take place at predefined periodic intervals.* |
| *Monitoring and reporting requires a time-based approach, whereas control (decision-making) is an event based activity.* |

*What this means*

How does the project board retain accountability for a project that they do not have the time to execute themselves? They delegate a stage at a time to an individual, the project manager, who then agrees to complete the stage within given constraints (stage-level tolerances). Progress information is sent to the project board at regular intervals confirming agreed progress via highlight reports (time-driven controls). If situations arise that pull the stage outside of the agreed constraints, there is a mechanism, exception reports (event-driven controls) in place to bring the project board up to date with the situation to make an informed decision about correcting it.

Event-driven controls are arrangements built into the project to ensure that things don't get 'out of control'. For example, the project is broken into management stages. At the end of each stage an end stage assessment is scheduled for the project board to consider the continuing viability of the project. It is a built-in arrangement to take a decision to continue (if things are under control) or stop (if things are not). Event-driven controls are instigated when an event occurs. If a stage is breaching one or more of its tolerances, an exception report is presented to the project board. If the stage has finished, an end stage assessment occurs. The events happening invoked the controls. Without the events, the controls would not occur.

Time-driven controls, those mechanisms put in place to occur periodically during the project to help monitor and report help the management of the project to stay on top of what is happening compared to what was planned to be happening. Highlight reports to the project board are time-driven controls about the progress of the stage. Checkpoint reports to the project manager are time-driven controls about the progress of a work package.

### *Illustration*

Patricia's project board set firm stage-level tolerances for her when they delegated her a management stage. As long as she was operating within these constraints, she had the authority to manage the stage on their behalf. The clear-cut constraints allowed Patricia to know her limits and understand when she needed to escalate exceptions, should they occur. On previous projects, there had always been an element of ambiguity that left a lot of grey area where things quickly got out of control. Although she didn't ever need to escalate any exceptions on her project, knowing the conditions that would cause this particular event-driven control helped her stay in control, make appropriate decisions and manage appropriately.

To help the project board understand the project's progress, they also asked Patricia to produce weekly highlight reports. The agreed timing was set for Friday afternoon to cover the week's progress to-date and confirm the next week's planned effort. These regular and recurring time-driven controls allowed the project board to see the project's progress as it occurred without having to be involved in at a detailed level.

Both event-driven and time-driven controls allowed Patricia's project board to use their time wisely. They didn't have to get involved in the day-to-day management, that was Patricia's job after all. And they didn't have to get involved in fixing things or making project decisions unless they were 'big enough' to warrant their attention, based on what they pre-determined as 'big enough'. They were controlling a project, without doing it themselves via a combination of control mechanisms delegated to and agreed with Patricia. Health check

| **Description:** |
| --- |
| *PRINCE2 provides process-oriented checklists that can be used at various points in the project to assess that the key aspects of PRINCE2 are adequately addressed.* |

## What this means

The health check offers a comprehensive question set that will help guide and inform an auditor or reviewer in finding strengths and weaknesses of a project. This tool can be used by project assurance when they want to perform a project review. Alternatively, the project manager may want to self-diagnose problem areas within his/her project. Even an outside expert wishing to conduct an official audit could use this tool. The starting point for the questions depends on how far the project has progressed through the process-based life cycle.

## Illustration

Harry was hired in as project assurance for the executive to work on their biggest project to date. The executive was too busy to understand why she was feeling so nervous about the project. She knew she didn't have much time to deal with the project manager, and was accepting everything he said at face value; but something was just not right. Harry, who had had years of experience managing successful projects, decided to start with a full assessment of the current situation. He asked the executive where they were in the project – the beginning, middle or end. He also asked the project manager the same thing. When he got two different answers, he realised there was an obvious communication gap. He broke out his PRINCE2 manual, started with Appendix E: Health check, and began asking questions.

This tool pulled out several key areas where the project management team was falling down. It was not just the project manager, but several of the inherent corporate or programme systems in place that were stopping the communication flows required for this large project. Without the health check, this project may have died a terrible death, taking personal and professional reputations down with it. As it was, Harry saved the day by using common sense and referring to best practice guidelines to find the problem.

# CHAPTER 13: TAILORING PRINCE2

## Tailoring successfully

| Description: |
| --- |
| *The goal (of tailoring) is to apply a level of project management that does not overburden the project management team but provides an appropriate level of governance and control, at an acceptable level of risk.*<br><br>*Tailoring is concerned with the appropriate use of PRINCE2 on any given project, ensuring that there is the right amount of governance, planning and control, in accordance with PRINCE2 principles.*<br><br>*Effective tailoring requires skill, experience and judgement.* |

### What this means

PRINCE2 is designed to be used with any project – big or small, simple or complex, part of a programme or stand-alone, in a single organisation or multi-organisational, an internal relationship or a commercial relationship, in the private sector or public sector, etc. No matter what the situation or arrangements for the project, considerations of how extensive and how formal PRINCE2 as a framework will be applied need to be made and understood by all interested parties. Without care, PRINCE2 can become overly bureaucratic for smaller, simpler projects. For larger, more complex projects there is a risk of developing a reputation of being "PRINCE2 in name only" (PINO).

Understanding the project's context, internal and external constraints will help tremendously to understand how PRINCE2 should be tailored for a project. There should be no question of tailoring the approach, as this is a mandatory principle to be applied to all projects - tailor to suit the project.

### *Illustration*

*Tailoring simple projects*

Helena had a 45-minute meeting with her boss (the executive) in a coffee shop to go over the basics of the project idea. When they were through, her boss authorised her to move into the initiating a project process. Helena documented the results of their discussion in a follow up email. For this small, simple and local project, an informal discussion between the executive and project manager was sufficient to cover all the points of the starting up a project process.

*Tailoring projects using an agile approach*

The nature of Ruth's project lent itself nicely to an agile approach as it had an immovable deadline. She tailored PRINCE2 to match the high-level of autonomy she would be delegating to her delivery team, allowing for flexibility with scope and quality criteria whilst hitting her strict deadlines. With the following adjustments she was able to take advantage of the benefits of staying in control that PRINCE2 provides as a structured method, yet also work in a flexible, agile manner.

Her plans reflected the need for timeboxes within each stage to iteratively develop proofs of concept, models and a working solution that could be moved into operational use through frequent releases. The role titles were modified to adjust for the different language used on an agile project. The accountabilities and responsibilities were moved around, but none were lost or dropped. The formality of the documentation was lessened to accommodate the speed of delivery and the need for more verbal communications within the agile environment. Flash cards with user stories took the place of product descriptions, a visible wall chart replaced team plans and daily stand-up meetings replaced checkpoint reports.

*Tailoring projects involving a commercial customer and supplier relationship*

When considering signing the contract to work with the customer on the project, Mario needed to consider everything before obligating his company. As the supplier, they would be held accountable for the quality of the specialist work. Was it defined clearly enough? Or were there vague areas that might result in conflict later in the project? As the supplier, they would be responsible for pre-contract activities (such as time and effort to provide a thorough response to the tender) and post-contract activities (such as ongoing maintenance work). Would these be paid for? Or were these assumed to be part of the overall price? As the supplier, they would be required to provide the specialist knowledge and expertise. How would this be utilised under the project's change control procedures? Was there a defined change control procedure? How would this affect the contract?

After all these considerations and more, Mario had to take the decision based on his beliefs that the overall cost-benefit analysis was worth the risk of legally committing to a contract with the customer. He needed to feel confident in the relationship between his company and the customer's. A thoroughly fleshed out PID would give him this confidence on how the customer planned to manage the project. And the contract would answer questions about compensation and dispute handling if this relationship dissolved.

*Tailoring projects involving multiple owning organisations*

Horace's new project involved partnership organisations, including the central government. Never having worked on such a massive and formal project before, it took Horace a while to figure out how to manage it appropriately. Very formal control mechanisms were put into place to keep a tight hold on all the facets of the project. With input from his own trial and error, advice from project assurance and lessons learned from previous large, organic projects, Horace developed a complete system with which he felt in control of the work instead of the work controlling him.

To start with, every project management team member signed an official role description to participate in the project. The original copy was held in the project's central files, another was given to the team members for their own reference, and a third was kept in their HR employee records file. This degree of formality ensured everyone completely understood their responsibilities in participating on the project team, as well as their authority limits and reporting lines within the project.

All management products, except for the exception report, were subjected to quality reviews with the project assurance staff members, before being sent to the project board. All management products sent to the project board were sent as hard copies and required two signatures – one for receipt and one for approval or rejection.

Horace became known throughout the multiple organisations as a well prepared and much admired mini dictator for the project, but he held that title in high regard. It was precisely because of these formalities that the large and often unwieldy project was kept in an efficient state throughout.

*Tailoring projects within programmes*

The programme above Lilian's project dictated to all of the projects, what systems they needed to use, all of the project's management approaches were pre-defined and the benefits in the business case were already identified and attached to her project's outcomes. The programme's PMO provided all the planning, risk, change control and quality expertise. All Lilian needed to do was operate within these constraints whilst managing her team to a successful project conclusion.

# CHAPTER 14: ROLES

## Project board

---

### Description:

*The project board is accountable to corporate, programme management or the customer for the success of the project, and has the authority to direct the project within the remit set by corporate, programme management or the customer as documented in the project mandate.*

*The project board is also responsible for the communications between the project management team and stakeholders external to that team (e.g. corporate programme management or the customer).*

---

### *What this means*

The project board members need to have enough authority within the organisation to make decisions about the project (for example, to authorise plans, allocate resources and represent their specific area – business, user or supplier). The members must demonstrate decision-making skills, leadership and commitment throughout the project. Ideally, the members will stay in their roles throughout the project's life.

### *Illustration*

*Project: Small, simple, local*

Joseph, the most senior manager of the department, took on the roles of executive, senior user and senior supplier for the project. He would also perform all the assurance activities for all three roles.

*Project: Large, complex, global*

Joanna, the most senior manager of the organisation, took on the role of executive. She appointed three other senior managers to fulfil the senior user role, and two senior managers to fulfil the senior supplier role – one internal and one external. The six members of the project board met formally at end-stage assessments and informally and/or virtually on a quarterly basis. Project assurance functions for all three project board roles were delegated to individuals in the quality assurance department, as well as to the internal finance manager, who was to perform additional business assurance.

### Executive

| Description: |
|---|
| *The executive is ultimately responsible for the project, supported by the senior user and senior supplier. The executive's role is to ensure that the project is focused throughout its life on achieving its objectives and delivering a product that will achieve the forecast benefits. The executive has to ensure that the project gives value for money, ensure a cost-conscious approach to the project, balancing the demands of the business, user and supplier.* |
| *Throughout the project, the executive is responsible for the business case.* |

> **The project board is not a democracy controlled by votes. The executive is the ultimate decision maker and is supported in the decision making by the senior user and senior supplier.**

## What this means

As the owner of the project, the executive takes on the most responsibility for the project. There can only be one executive on a project team. If there are two or more people fulfilling this role, there will be guaranteed confusion, misdirection and frustration. For true ownership to exist, only one person can assume accountability – one person whose neck is on the line. If the project was to go horribly wrong due to poor project management, it would not be the project manager who got blamed, but the executive (even in a no-blame environment). How could they have let the project go on and on without the requisite project management skills, resources and funding in place? If the project was to go horribly wrong due to other reasons (for example, economic, environmental, societal or technological changes) then there should be no one to blame. It would be up to the executive to either close the project prematurely or escalate the situation to corporate, programme management or the customer.

Because the executive appoints the project board members, the board members are accountable to him/her. They may be peers of the executive in their line management jobs, but, on the project management team, they are supporting functions to aid the executive in decision-making for the best interests of the project. The executive will arrange the project funding and chair the project board meetings.

The executive has responsibility for the function of business assurance. They may delegate this to any group or individual, except for the project manager.

### *Illustration*

*Project: Small, simple, local*

Jackie, the CEO of a small, privately-held business, appointed herself as executive for a small project. Even though the project was small in scale, she felt, as head of the company, she was in the best position to ensure that the project provided value for money. Additionally, Jackie planned on fulfilling the project assurance roles by mentoring the project manager and reviewing their work regularly.

*Project: Large, complex, global*

Jack, the CEO of a large multinational organisation, took ownership of the project because of its importance to the future of the organisation and his personal desire to ensure it contributed to the bottom line by expanding the business and profits. His strong belief in the project idea and the potential for the organisation's future drove him to seek out and arrange funding from creative sources, such as partnership agreements, grants and the issuing of common stocks. With the aid of the finance director and legal counsel performing business assurance at every step of the way, Jack was guaranteed a sound business investment in the project.

**Senior user**

| Description: |
| :---: |
| *The senior user(s) is responsible for specifying the needs of those who will use the project's products, for user liaison with the project management team, and for monitoring that the solution will meet those needs within the constraints of the business case in terms of quality, functionality and ease of use.* |
| *The role represents the interests of all those who will use the project's products (including operations and maintenance), those for whom the products will achieve an objective or those who will use the products to deliver benefits. The senior user role commits user resources and monitors products against requirements. The role may require more than one person to cover all the user interests. For the sake of effectiveness, the role should not be split between too many people.* |

*What this means*

Someone in management from the customer organisation needs to represent the user interests throughout the project. The users will be those groups or individuals who will use or be impacted by the project's products. The senior user will ensure, from a management perspective, that the products are being created, tested and approved with the users in mind. Additionally, the products will need to be usable for them to be used. The only way to get benefits from a project is for the users to change their behaviour (the outcome) by using the project's products (the outputs). The senior user will thus help specify and define the projects, and will be held accountable for their realisation, even after the project concludes.

The senior user has responsibility for the function of user assurance. They may delegate this to any group or individual, except for the project manager.

### *Illustration*

*Project: Small, simple, local*

Guillermo put his name into the pot to be the senior user for the new automated phone system project. He currently supervises the team of call centre staff who will be trialling the new system for the company. He has progressed his career through the ranks, so feels he is in an excellent position to understand the needs of his staff and what is in their best interests.

*Project: Large, complex, global*

Willamina runs the directorate that will be most impacted by the project. She has insisted, from the beginning, that she be on the project board in the role of senior user. She shares this role with the director of sales and the director of market research. Together, they represent the internal staff and end users worldwide. As directors in the organisation, they recognise that they are too busy to fulfil their own project assurance, and have each delegated this responsibility to one or more middle managers within their directorates. Additionally, their project assurance delegates will also form a global user group to take in ideas and feedback about the project. This information will be collected and fed back to the three senior users to help them in their formal role representing the user community.

## Senior supplier

> ### Description:
>
> *The senior supplier represents the interests of those designing, developing, facilitating, procuring and implementing the project's products. This role is accountable for the quality of products delivered by the supplier(s) and is responsible for the technical integrity of the project. If necessary, more than one person may be required to represent the suppliers.*
>
> *Depending on the particular customer/supplier environment, the customer may also wish to appoint an independent person or group to carry out assurance on the supplier's products (for example, if the relationship between the customer and supplier is a commercial one).*

### What this means

Someone in management from either the customer and/or an external supplier organisation needs to represent the supplier interests throughout the project. The suppliers are those individuals or groups of specialist and technical workers who will supply the project's specialist products. Typically, under business as usual conditions, the senior supplier is the line manager above the suppliers. They will be held accountable for the quality of products supplied by the suppliers.

The senior supplier has responsibility for the function of supplier assurance. They may delegate this to any group or individual, except for the project manager.

## *Illustration*

### *Project: Small, simple, local*

Charles is the account manager at a small web design firm. He has two designers working on the front-end interface for the new website ordered by the client. He will represent the web design firm's interests during the two-month project.

### *Project: Large, complex, global*

Chelsea is the top sales executive for IGM Financial Inc. As IGM is the major supplier for the client's new bespoke IGM-based international investment system, Chelsea is performing the senior supplier role. She will share this role with other major suppliers internal and external to the client organisation. As the lead supplier, however, she will also chair a separate supplier group of all the suppliers. They will meet monthly to discuss technical aspects of the project, and Chelsea will ensure that they stay coordinated and efficient in their efforts.

## Project manager

---

### Description:

***The project manager has the authority to run the project on a day-to-day basis on behalf of the project board within the constraints laid down by them.***

***The project manager's prime responsibility is to ensure that the project produces the required products within the specified tolerances of time, cost, quality, scope, risk and benefits. The project manager is also responsible for the project producing a result of achieving benefits defined in the business case.***

---

## What this means

The project manager reports to and takes direction from the project board. They have the day-to-day control over the project for a management stage at a time. As long as they are inside – and predicted to remain inside – the stage-level tolerances, they have authority to make decisions about the management stage. To maintain control over the management stage without actually doing the work, the project manager must be good at people management, communications, negotiation and delegation.

## Illustration

### Project: Small, simple, local

Stephanie is a full-time project manager. She currently manages four small projects within her organisation. Two of her projects are ending soon, so she feels she can take on another one. This new one is also quite small and within her area of expertise, so she feels it will be a good fit and good timing.

### Project: Large, complex, global

Steven is a full-time project manager dedicated to one project. He has two junior managers assisting him with his management responsibilities, as well as a project support team that oversees the project's administration duties. To stay on top of the project, Steven meets with his assistants and the rest of project support every morning for a brief 20-minute update meeting on Skype®. The only rule for the meeting is that there are no rules. Anything can be surfaced. However, agenda items requiring more time and attention will be dealt with offline, in separate meetings. Managing the project management this way, Steven feels that he is fostering an environment that is open and transparent, so issues will not be hidden.

## Team manager

---

**Description:**

*The team manager's prime responsibility is to ensure production of those products defined by the project manager to an appropriate quality, in a set timescale and at a cost acceptable to the project board. The team manager role reports to, and takes direction from, the project manager.*

---

### *What this means*

The individuals performing the team manager role within a project are the specialist and technical experts who either produce the project's specialist products or manage the team members who do. The team manager takes responsibility for the product creation as agreed in the work package. They ensure that the quality-checking activities planned for the products are carried out correctly, with the results updated in the quality register. While creating the products, the team manager sends regular progress information to the project manager via checkpoint reports. All finished work is handed back to the project manager in the fashion and manner agreed in the work package.

### *Illustration*

*Project: Small, simple, local*

Pollyanna has recently earned her PhD degree in her highly specialised field. Her extensive knowledge in this field positions her well to be an ideal candidate for the team manager role. However, her work experience is quite limited. So, to start her off and introduce her to the culture, limitations and constraints of her new corporate environment, her new manager has asked her to use her skills on a small project. Her small team has been in the organisation for some time, and will help her adjust to the move from academia to commerciality.

For every piece of specialist work that Pollyanna and her team attempts, Pollyanna first agrees the work and the constraints with a project manager. For up until she and her team have fully gelled as a team, Pollyanna has set an indiscriminate, temporary limit of three work packages that she and her team will take on at any point in time. As the work progresses in each of the work packages, Pollyanna checks in with her team members and then sends checkpoint reports via email to the various project managers. Finally, as each piece of work is completed, she sends the completed products back to the project managers, usually by walking them over to their offices next door.

## Project: Large, complex, global

Pier Paolo is one of 15 team managers working on the project during this management stage. His role is to manage the co-located team in Portugal, Spain and southern France. He meets with his team members in person on a weekly basis, and gets daily feedback from them via email. He regularly speaks with two other team managers who are working on related products in other regions. He provides weekly checkpoint reports via email to the project manager, in which he gives updates about his progress according to his team plan. So far, he has only had to raise one issue about a small delay that took him out of his work package tolerances. The issue was resolved by the project manager, who gave him extra time tolerance to cover the delay.

**Project assurance**

---

### Description:

*Project assurance covers the primary stakeholder interests (business, user and supplier).*

*Project assurance has to be independent of the project manager; therefore, the project board cannot delegate any of its assurance activities to the project manager.*

---

### *What this means*

Technically, project assurance is not a separate role, but a function or responsibility of the project board members. If the project board members find that they are too busy or do not have the required skills to fulfil this function, they can delegate it to an individual or group of individuals, as long as the person or group is independent of the project manager.

The purpose of the project assurance is to review, check and advise the project manager (along with project support and the team managers) in their performance of managing the project. Specialist products will be checked and reviewed by objective specialists in well-defined quality reviews. Management products need to be checked and reviewed by objective persons carrying out the project assurance function covering the business, user and supplier perspectives. Because this function exists as an integral part of the PRINCE2 framework, the project board can rest assured that any information they receive from the project manager has been reviewed or checked first by project assurance.

## *Illustration*

### *Project: Small, simple, local*

Marcia is the executive, senior user and senior supplier for the project. She has decided to perform all her project assurance responsibilities. Over the next six weeks – the length of the project – it is not worth bringing in and paying for extra resources to perform these duties, which she truly believes she will have time to take on. It will be tight, of course, and require some overtime on her part, but for this short project, she feels this is the best solution.

### *Project: Large, complex, global*

Marcus performs the user assurance activities for the senior user of the project. He reviews all the product descriptions, including the project product description from the user perspectives. He checks that they accurately reflect the true purpose of the products and examines the quality criteria and tolerances to ensure they are within acceptable limits for the users. Marcus advises the project manager on who should be chosen as an appropriate reviewer to test the products when they are complete. He reports regularly to the senior users, assuring them that the project manager is doing quality work and focusing on creating usable products. Finally, Marcus also liaises with the two other individuals who are performing user assurance to take care that they do not step on each other's responsibilities, overload the project manager, or, worse yet, provide conflicting guidance to the project manager.

Manuela performs similar tasks on behalf of the executive of the project. Her focus, however, is to advise and review project work to ensure that the project remains focused on achieving its objectives and delivering products that will achieve the benefits. To do this, she assists the project manager in developing the business case and benefits management approach. Her typical duties involve verifying, checking and reviewing the financial aspects of the project, all the while focusing on the continued viability of the project.

Finally, Monte has been assigned to perform supplier assurance for the same project. His expertise in writing requirements comes in handy when he must review product descriptions that detail quality criteria for each of the project's specialist products. His responsibilities centre on advising and monitoring the management of the product creation from start to finish. He not only reviews how the products have been described in product descriptions, but also advises on the right method(s) to create the products. Additionally, he assesses whether the quality control methods will, in fact, correctly test that the products meet their quality criteria.

**Change authority**

---

**Description:**

*The project board may delegate authority for approving responses to requests for change or off-specifications to a separate individual or group, called a change authority. The project manager could be assigned as the change authority for some aspects of the project (e.g. changing*

---

> *baselined work packages if it does not affect management stage tolerances).*

## What this means

Technically, change authority is not a separate role, but a function or responsibility of the project board members. If the project board members find that they are too busy or do not have the required technical skills to fulfil this function, they can delegate it to an individual or group of individuals, including the project manager.

The purpose of the change authority is to review and approve or reject all requests for change and off-specifications (missing or incomplete products). The change authority function can be split and divided among many individuals if the technical complexity of the project calls for it. If a change budget is created, the change authority may use this within their delegated limits for approving changes. Sometimes, the best person to review and approve or reject a change is the person who is currently working on the product being impacted: the team manager. If the project board feels that a certain team manager has the right skill sets, or they trust his/her judgment about changes, they can pass part or all of their change authority function to him/her.

## Illustration

*Project: Small, simple, local*

Tony is the project manager, project support and team manager for his project. His boss (the executive) has delegated most of the change authority function to him, as well. He is authorised to make decisions about changes up to a £1,000 limit at a time. His total change budget is £15,000. Any change(s) requiring more than £1,000 at a time, or causing the spend to exceed the total change budget of £15,000, will call for Tony to escalate the change to his boss.

*Project: Large, complex, global*

Tawnya sits on a design board within her organisation. The design board contributes their extensive technical and specialist knowledge and expertise to the project as the change authority. Impact analyses of requests for change and off-specifications require in-depth investigations and comprehensive understandings of the intricacies of the organisation's existing and future systems. Tawnya and the design board assist the project manager with these analytical examinations and propose options for dealing with the potentially complicated modifications. Then, as a group, they decide on the best approach.

**Project support**

| Description: |
| --- |
| *The provision of any project support on a formal basis is optional. If it is not delegated to a separate person or function it will need to be undertaken by the project manager.* |
| *One support function that must be considered is that of change control. Depending on the project size and environment, there may be a need to formalise this and it may become a task with which the project manager cannot cope without support.* |

## What this means

The larger and more complex a project is, the bigger the need for a separate person or people to fulfil the project support role. Project support aids with the project administration. They must have administrative skills, be organised, and pay attention to detail. Collecting information and keeping records up to date is a primary function, especially for change control over the project's management and specialist products.

## Illustration

*Project: Small, simple, local*

Helena worked on the project team as project support for 10% of her time. This meant she spent, on average, four hours a week ensuring that records were up to date, filed in the right place and correctly labelled. Periodically, she attended project meetings. There, she took the minutes, but mostly, she filed documents, stored specialist products in a cupboard, and emailed reports to defined distribution lists.

*Project: Large, complex, global*

Ellen managed a support team of 20 staff members. Together, they supported two programmes and five stand-alone projects. Their duties included workshop facilitation, and mentoring of project managers – especially in planning tools, estimating methods and change control. Their well-defined systems and expertise in organisation kept the most up-to-date information flowing to the right people at the right times.

# CHAPTER 15: MANAGEMENT PRODUCTS

> *Management products are not necessarily documents, they are information sets that are used by the PRINCE2 processes, so that certain roles can take action and/or make decisions.*

## Tailoring management products

> **Note:**
>
> *Management products should be tailored to the requirements and environment of each project. This could include the composition, format, quality criteria and naming of the management products.*

### *Illustration*

*Project: Small, simple, local*

Shannon's project was relatively small and straightforward. She was not only the project manager, but the team manager and project support. She agreed with her executive that the project documentation set would be light and informal, most of which would be captured in her project notebook - her daily log.

*Project: Large, complex, global*

Sherwyn's project was part of a large programme which itself was constrained by strict industry standards and subjected to regular and frequent audits. He was required to use the company's exhaustive and thorough templates for capturing and documenting project information, storing them in company approved systems and limiting access rights based on his company's confidentiality procedures. Additionally, the PRINCE2 management product titles were adjusted to better match the industry standards and programme processes.

The following list of management products is in alphabetical order.

**Benefits management approach**

---

**PURPOSE:**

*A benefits management approach defines the benefits management actions and benefits reviews that will be put in place to ensure that the project's outcomes are achieved and confirm that the project's benefits are realised.*

---

*When is it created? When is it updated?*

- Created during the initiating a project process
- Updated during the managing a stage boundary and closing a project processes, or – when requested by the project board via ad hoc direction – using the project's formal change control procedures.

*Illustration*

*Project: Small, simple, local*

Based on the executive's request, Obe's benefits management approach was not a separate document, but rather an additional section in the business case, listing the proposed dates and measures for all the benefits justifying the project to be assessed.

*Project: Large, complex, global*

Onawara created an extensive benefits management approach, which explained how and when each of the project's benefits should be measured post-project. Her detailed instructions included resource requirements needed for the measurements and the desired skill sets to perform the reviews.

**Business case**

---

### PURPOSE:

*A business case is used to document the justification for the undertaking of a project, based on the estimated costs (of development, implementation and incremental ongoing operations and maintenance costs) against the anticipated benefits to be gained and offset by any associated risks.*

---

*When is it created? When is it updated?*

- Created in outline form during the starting up a project process
- Created fully during the initiating a project process
- Updated during the managing a stage boundary and closing a project processes, or – when requested by the project board via ad hoc direction – using the project's formal change control procedures.

*Illustration*

*Project: Small, simple, local*

Sheila's outline business case was a section of her project brief, which was captured on the back of a serviette. Her full business case was more formal than that. It was captured in an email to her boss, along with the other considerations for the project initiation documentation.

*Project: Large, complex, global*

Shawn's business case covered ten sides of A4 paper, and fully documented and described the benefits, drawbacks, timescales, costs and major risks. It was distributed to the 17 senior managers within the organisation for review, and only approved after external scrutiny from a financial advisor.

**Change control approach**

| PURPOSE: |
|---|
| *A change control approach is used to identify, assess and control any potential and approved changes to the project baselines. It describes the procedures, techniques and standards to be applied and the responsibilities for achieving an effective issue management and change control procedure.* |

*When is it created? When is it updated?*

- Created during the initiating a project process
- If required, updated during the managing a stage boundary process.

*Illustration*

*Project: Small, simple, local*

Lolita captured issues and changes on a Microsoft Excel spreadsheet. At the end of each day, she reviewed them looking at the possible options, and then decided on the best one(s). Lolita had change authority responsibilities, made the decisions about requests for change and escalated any exceptions to the project board immediately, first through a phone call, then backed up with an email.

*Project: Large, complex, global*

Damien and his global team used a complex, bespoke software on his project called COMPANYX-PROJECT-ISSUE. His PMO had dedicated staff to review and analyse issues as they were entered. An existing Change Authority Board (CAB) made decisions about changes. Issues inside stage-level tolerance were referred back to Damien and exceptions outside stage-level tolerance were directed to the project board. The sophistication of the software and the PMO infrastructure allowed for Damien to concentrate on managing his team and dealing with issues under his control whilst allowing the organisation's expertise to coordinate and control the wider issue and change control procedures.

**Checkpoint report**

| **PURPOSE:** |
| --- |
| *A checkpoint report is used to report, at a frequency defined in the work package, the status of the work package.* |

*When is it created? When is it updated?*

- Created during the managing product delivery process
- Not updated – new reports are created to provide updated progress information.

## *Illustration*

### *Project: Small, simple, local*

Scarlett, the team manager, leaned over her desk and told Johan, the project manager, that she was almost finished with one thing and about to start on another. Johan noted it in his notebook (the daily log).

### *Project: Large, complex, global*

Seamus personally interviewed every member of his team to find out the statuses of their products, and what issues, risks and concerns they had. He marked their progress on his team plan, wrote up a report using the approved checkpoint report template, and sent it to the project manager, copying in project support and project assurance.

### Communication management approach

> ### PURPOSE:
>
> *A communication management approach contains a description of the means and frequency of communication to parties both internal and external to the project. It facilitates engagement with stakeholders through the establishment of a controlled and bidirectional flow of information.*

### *When is it created? When is it updated?*

- Created during the initiating a project process
- If required, updated during the managing a stage boundary process.

## *Illustration*

### *Project: Small, simple, local*

Ethan referenced the corporate communication management approach and noted that all project team communication between himself and the executive would most likely be verbal, and backed up with emails stored in his email system.

### *Project: Large, complex, global*

Abby referenced the corporate communication strategy and documented the variances her project would be making to accommodate the 15 external suppliers, the tools they would be using, and the intricate feedback loop mechanism designed especially for this project. All stakeholders were identified and analysed by local or regional teams to provide the most insight and cultural nuances possible.

## Configuration item record

| PURPOSE: |
| :---: |
| *Configuration item records are only created if required by the project's change control approach. Their purpose is to provide a record of such information as the history, status, version and variant of each configuration item, and any details of important relationships between them. The set of configuration item records for a project is often referred to as a configuration library.* |

## When is it created? When is it updated?

- If required by the project's change control approach, created as soon as the need for a product has been identified, usually as part of a planning exercise
- Updated during the controlling a stage, managing product delivery, managing a stage boundary and closing a project processes.

## *Illustration*

*Project: Small, simple, local*

Dalia kept a Microsoft Excel spreadsheet that tracked the five criteria for the seven main products of her project.

She tracked:

1. Unique item identifiers
2. Version numbers
3. Statuses
4. Relationships with each other
5. Any issue numbers that caused changes to the products.

Dalia was the project manager, team manager and the project support for this project. For this reason, she didn't need to track anything else; as she would be the one to own the products, they'd be in her office and worked on only during the one subsequent management stage of the project.

*Project: Large, complex, global*

Leonard used a database to keep track of 50 separate criteria for his project's products. Access to the database was limited to authorised support staff to ensure tight control over the information. The number of changes to a single item per day could run in the hundreds.

## Daily log

> ### PURPOSE:
>
> *A daily log may be used to record informal issues, required actions or significant events not caught by other PRINCE2 registers or logs. It can act as the project diary for the project manager.*

### When is it created? When is it updated?

- Created during the starting up a project process
- Updated during the initiating a project, controlling a stage, managing a stage boundary and closing a project processes by the project manager
- If the team manager also uses a daily log, then it is created and updated during the managing product delivery process.

### *Illustration*

*Project: Small, simple, local*

Fabienne – fulfilling the roles of project manager, team manager and project support – used her daily log as her combined daily log, lessons log, issue register, risk register and quality register throughout the project.

*Project: Large, complex, global*

Jacob used a 200-page loose-leaf binder as his daily log. He captured everything in it – from conversations to ideas, thoughts, concerns and observations about the project. He reviewed his daily log every two hours to ensure that he transferred his notes to the appropriate management product. Although he liked to use paper, he requested that his team managers use personal digital assistance (PDAs) that would link into his computer, so he could review their notes and see if he needed to add them to any formal project documentation.

**End project report**

> **PURPOSE:**
>
> *An end project report is used during project closure to review how the project performed against the version of the PID used to authorise it. It also allows the:*
>
> - *Passing on of any lessons that can be usefully applied to other projects*
> - *Passing on of details of unfinished work, ongoing risks or potential product modifications to the group charged with future support of the project's products in their operational life.*

*When is it created? When is it updated?*

- Created during the closing a project process – either as part of a planned or premature closure
- Not updated.

*Illustration*

*Project: Small, simple, local*

Paco reviewed the project initiation documentation, which had been created six weeks earlier, and compared the final product with it. There were some minor differences, which he explained by reviewing the risk and issue registers. He summed up his findings in an email to the project executive (the end project report).

*Project: Large, complex, global*

Yancey and four members of her team spent five full days preparing to write the end project report. They reviewed the original PID, which had been created by Yancy's predecessor six years ago, and then combed through the various revised versions updated throughout the project. After a thorough appraisal, Yancey was able to give a complete assessment of the project efforts (the end project report).

## End-stage report

| **PURPOSE:** |
| --- |
| *An end-stage report is used to give a summary of progress to date, the overall situation, and sufficient information to ask for a project board decision on what to do next with the project.* |

## When is it created? When is it updated?

- Created during the managing a stage boundary process
- Not updated: new reports are issued at the end of every subsequent management stage, except for the final one; an end project report is issued at the end of the final stage.

## *Illustration*

### *Project: Small, simple, local*

Balthasar recapped his initiation stage experience as his one and only end-stage report, and sent it in an email to the executive. He did not need to write another one for his project, as there was only one subsequent management stage. At the end of that management stage, he would write the end project report.

### *Project: Large, complex, global*

Warren reviewed his previous highlight reports from this management stage and cut and pasted any relevant information into his end-stage report. He added the finishing touches about the last piece of work and his assessment of how the management stage went. He pulled a stage-level status accounting report to prove all the products from this management stage had, in fact, been completed, tested and approved. He then sent this information to project assurance to review, before sending it on to the project board for approval.

### Exception report

| PURPOSE: |
| :---: |
| *An exception report is produced when a stage plan or project plan is forecast to exceed tolerance levels set. It is prepared by the project manager in order to inform the project board of the situation, and to offer options and recommendations for the way to proceed.* |

## When is it created? When is it updated?

- Created during the controlling a stage process, when the stage-level tolerances are forecast to be exceeded
- Updated as decisions and resolutions are confirmed and implemented regarding the exception.

## Illustration

### Project: Small, simple, local

Nadia picked up the phone and dialled the number of her boss (who was also the project's executive). She gave a quick rundown of the exception situation and a brief recap of the ideas she had to deal with it. She also confirmed that she would now sit down and send this information to her again via email, but needed to give her boss the immediate heads-up first.

### Project: Large, complex, global

Masood had been reviewing the impact of the issue with three members of project assurance to get the best estimates of how big the problem was. The issue had been captured by one of his team managers, who entered it in a formal issue report. It was now evident that Masood would have to escalate this issue via an exception report. He telephoned the executive to give him an early verbal warning, and then created the formal exception report. He then distributed it to the entire project board, as well as to other members from corporate and programme management who, as indicated in the communication approach, needed to be kept in the loop of exception situations.

## Highlight report

---

**PURPOSE:**

*A highlight report is used to provide the project board (and possibly other stakeholders) with a summary of the management stage status at intervals defined by them. The project board uses the report to monitor management stage and project progress. The project manager also uses it to advise the project board of any potential problems or areas where the project board could help.*

---

### When is it created? When is it updated?

- Created during the controlling a stage process and at the frequency defined by the project board
- Not updated – new reports are created to provide updated progress information.

### Illustration

*Project: Small, simple, local*

Janice, the project manager, had her weekly one-on-one manager meeting with her boss, the executive. She included progress information (a highlight report) about the three projects she was managing.

*Project: Large, complex, global*

With the aid of her project support team, Zelda reviewed and assessed all the checkpoint reports from the team managers to glean the highlights to report to the project board. They looked through the issue, risk and quality registers to find any new items worth including in the reporting. They double-checked the product checklist to ensure all the products listed for this period had been completed. The highlight report was then assembled, reviewed by project assurance for accuracy, and then sent on to the project board and other interested stakeholders identified on the communication management approach.

## Issue register

---

### PURPOSE:

*The purpose of the issue register is to capture and maintain information on all the issues that are being formally managed. The issue register should be monitored by the project manager on a regular basis.*

---

### *When is it created? When is it updated?*

- Created during the initiating a project process; any issues identified earlier will be transferred from the daily log to the issue register
- Updated during the initiating a project, controlling a stage, managing a stage boundary and closing a project processes.

### *Illustration*

*Project: Small, simple, local*

Nora – fulfilling the roles of project manager, team manager and project support – used her daily log as her issue register throughout the project.

*Project: Large, complex, global*

Philip created a bespoke web-enabled issue register database that could be accessed by all team members around the world. Entry into the register was no longer restricted by time zones. Any team member anywhere in the world could make an entry. Project support reviewed the database four times a day and called the author(s) if there were any questions. Philip assessed the new entries every day for at least one hour, taking corrective action where he had the authority to do so, or escalating them (in an exception report) where he did not.

**Issue report**

---

### PURPOSE:

*An issue report is a report containing the description, impact assessment and recommendations for a request for change, off-specification or problem/concern. It is only created for those issues that need to be handled formally.*

---

*When is it created? When is it updated?*

- Created at any time from the initiation stage onwards, where an issue has been identified that needs to be formally managed. If authority has been delegated to the team manager to use the issue report, then they would create one during the managing product delivery process. Otherwise, the project manager will create them during the initiating a project and controlling a stage processes.
- Updated as decisions and resolutions are confirmed and implemented regarding the issue during the initiating a project, controlling a stage, managing a stage boundary and closing a project processes.

### *Illustration*

#### *Project: Small, simple, local*

Wendy used email to capture formal issues that she wanted to get to the attention of the project board (her boss). The threaded email discussions also captured the final decisions made. Wendy was also able to use the dates and times on the emails to organise and arrange the issues in a folder on her desktop.

#### *Project: Large, complex, global*

Francis used the programme's official issue report template to capture issues. When authorising work packages to his team managers, he included the template for them to use as well. Project support used a document management system to track and store all the issue reports from the project. Project assurance checked and reviewed the reports to make sure that all the team members were using the correct and latest version of the template.

### Lessons log

---

### PURPOSE:

*The lessons log is a project repository for lessons that apply to this project or future projects. Some lessons may originate from other projects and should be captured on the lessons log for input to the project's approaches and plans. Some lessons may originate from within the project, where new experience (both good and bad) can be passed to others.*

---

### When is it created? When is it updated?

- Created during the starting up a project process
- Updated whenever a lesson is learned, or, at the very least, at the end of each management stage during the managing a stage boundary and closing a project processes.

### Illustration

*Project: Small, simple, local*

Farrah – fulfilling the roles of project manager, team manager and project support – used her daily log to capture lessons throughout the project.

*Project: Large, complex, global*

Michael had monthly meetings with his team managers and members of project assurance to ensure they were capturing lessons as they progressed through the project. Many of the lessons were learned through risks and issues experienced on the project and reflections on how these could have been predicted more accurately or avoided through better planning. The lessons log was filed with the official project documentation administered by project support. Any new lessons identified in their review meetings were added to the log by project support, cross-referencing the risk register or issue register where appropriate.

## Lessons report

---

### PURPOSE:

*The lessons report is used to pass on any lessons that can be usefully applied to other projects.*

*The purpose of the report is to provoke action, so that the positive lessons become embedded in the organisation's way of working, and that the organisation is able to avoid any negative lessons on future projects.*

---

### *When is it created? When is it updated?*

- Created at any time, but typically is done during the managing a stage boundary and/or closing a project processes
- Not updated – new reports may be issued when major or important lessons need to be distributed and shared with the rest of the organisation.

### *Illustration*

*Project: Small, simple, local*

Kaelem reserved an agenda item in the final project meeting to discuss the ups and downs of the project experience with his team. He captured the sentiments in the meeting minutes (the lessons report) and distributed these to the executive and other project managers in his department.

*Project: Large, complex, global*

Annie and her team wrote a comprehensive lessons report, which they shared with the project board and key stakeholders identified in the communication management approach. The report was translated into six different languages and revised to meet the needs of local and regional cultures and customs, so that it could be shared around the entire organisation. Another modified version was distributed to key suppliers who had additional, ongoing business relationships with the organisation.

**Plan**

---

**PURPOSE:**

*A plan provides a statement of how and when objectives are to be achieved, by showing the major products, activities and resources required for the scope of the plan. In PRINCE2, there are three levels of plan: project, stage and team. Team plans are optional.*

*A plan should cover the activities to manage product creation, including activities for assurance, quality management, risk management, change control, communication and any other project controls required.*

---

*When is it created? When is it updated?*

- Project plan
  - ○ Created during the initiating a project process
  - ○ Updated during the managing a stage boundary and closing a project processes
- Stage plan or exception plan
  - ○ Created during the starting up a project and managing a stage boundary processes
  - ○ Updated during the controlling a stage and closing a project processes

- Team plan
    - If created, created during the managing product delivery process
    - If created, updated during the managing product delivery process.

### *Illustration*

*Project: Small, simple, local*

For his one subsequent management stage project, Iago's project plan was also his stage plan. No team plans were required, as he was not only the project manager, but also the team manager.

*Project: Large, complex, global*

Gabriella's project plan and stage plans comprised of one version created using specialised planning software, a presentation version in Microsoft PowerPoint®, and a product checklist version in Microsoft Word®. To keep consistent records on progress, she required her team managers to use the same specialised planning software, but left it up to each team manager to determine if they required a presentational version and/or product checklist.

**Product description**

| PURPOSE: |
|---|
| *A product description is used to:* |
| • *Understand the detailed nature, purpose, function and appearance of the product* |
| • *Define who will use the product* |

> - ***Identify the sources of information or supply for the product***
> - ***Identify the level of quality required of the product***
> - ***Enable identification of activities to produce, review and approve the product***
> - ***Define the people or skills required to produce, review and approve the product.***

## *When is it created? When is it updated?*

- Created as soon as the need for a product has been identified. High-level products are identified in the project plan during the initiating a project process. Lower-level products are identified in the stage plan made during the managing a stage boundary process. Even smaller component products may require product descriptions for the team plan, which is created during the managing product delivery process.
- Not updated – approved product descriptions are subject to the project's formal change control procedures.

## *Illustration*

*Project: Small, simple, local*

Mackenzie – fulfilling the roles of project manager, team manager and project support – used her daily log to capture the requirements of the three main products she was required to create for her project.

*Project: Large, complex, global*

Lindsey used a bespoke requirements-capturing software package to define and analyse her project's products. The system was able to translate her product descriptions into up to 70 different languages and regional dialects.

**Product status account**

> ## PURPOSE:
>
> *If required by the project's change control approach, a product status account is used to provide information about the state of products within defined limits. The limits can vary. For example, the report could cover the entire project, a particular management stage, a particular area of the project, or the history of a specific product. It is particularly useful if the project manager wishes to confirm the version number of products.*

*When is it created? When is it updated?*

- Created at any time after configuration item records have been created. The status account report will reflect all the statuses of the products defined for the report: i.e. managing a stage boundary and closing a project
- Not updated – later versions of the report may be pulled at later times.

*Illustration*

*Project: Small, simple, local*

Lakeisha was able to print her Microsoft Excel® spreadsheet of her configuration item records at any point in time. This printed version acted as her product status account report.

*Project: Large, complex, global*

Horace required specialised reporting software to define and create his product status account reports. The software helped Horace set the reporting constraints from dropdown menus – such as the product's type, language, country of origin, status, version, management stage, owner, etc. It also allowed him to filter the report by date ranges.

**Project brief**

| PURPOSE: |
|---|
| *A project brief is used to provide a full and firm foundation for the initiation of the project and is created in the starting up a project process.* |

*When is it created? When is it updated?*

- Created during the starting up a project process
- Not updated – information from the project brief may be expanded and refined in the PID, after which the project brief is no longer maintained.

*Illustration*

*Project: Small, simple, local*

Shelley's project brief was never actually written down. It was the result of her discussions with her manager, the project board executive.

*Project: Large, complex, global*

Ladarius's project brief was presented to him by the programme manager. It stipulated the programme's aims and how this project fitted in with them. It provided a wealth of information about how the project was expected to run and the project constraints and tolerances being allocated to it.

**Project initiation documentation (PID)**

| **PURPOSE:** |
|---|
| *The purpose of the PID is to define the project, in order to form the basis for its management and an assessment of its overall success. The project initiation documentation gives the direction and scope of the project and (along with the stage plan) forms the "contract" between the project manager and the project board.* |

*When is it created? When is it updated?*

- Assembled during the initiating a project process. Information inside the PID is created throughout the starting up a project and initiating a project processes
- If required, updated during the managing a stage boundary process, or when requested by the project board via ad hoc direction using the project's formal change control procedures.

*Illustration*

*Project: Small, simple, local*

Serena held a formal one-day meeting with her manager (the project board executive) with a detailed agenda. The agenda covered all the points required for the project initiation documentation. All the requisite decisions were made and captured in the meeting. Serena used the meeting minutes as the documented PID, and had her boss formally approve it via email confirmation.

*Project: Large, complex, global*

Vanessa worked with six members of her team over a period of three and a half months to produce the project's PID. They had countless consultations with project assurance, the project board members themselves and external experts while creating the right level of documentation to help manage and control the massive change effort successfully.

**Project product description**

---

**PURPOSE:**

*The project product description is a special form of product description that defines what the project must deliver in order to gain acceptance. It is used to:*

- *Gain agreement from the user on the project's scope and requirements*
  - *Define the customer's quality expectations*
  - *Define the acceptance criteria, method and responsibilities for the project.*

---

*When is it created? When is it updated?*

- Created as part of the project brief during the starting up a project process
- Created in full during the initiating a project process
- If required, updated during the managing a stage boundary or – when requested by the project board via

ad hoc direction – using the project's formal change control procedures.

## *Illustration*

### *Project: Small, simple, local*

Amanda – fulfilling the roles of project manager, team manager and project support – kept a picture of the final product on the wall of her office. She kept this in plain view, so that she would always focus on delivering exactly that.

### *Project: Large, complex, global*

Marjorie's project product description evolved over several major scoping exercises with the user groups, supplier groups, project board members and legal representation from several countries. After negotiations about what was desired, what was possible, and what was legal and achievable, a working project product description was finally agreed. The final version demonstrated several key compromises on how it would be ultimately accepted by the senior users at the end of the project.

## Quality management approach

---

**PURPOSE:**

*A quality management approach is used to define the quality techniques and standards to be applied, and the various responsibilities for achieving the required quality levels, during the project.*

---

**When is it created? When is it updated?**

- Created during the initiating a project process
- If required, updated during the managing a stage boundary process.

***Illustration***

*Project: Small, simple, local*

Taylor referenced her corporate quality management system and noted that her colleague, Bill, would quality review all seven of the project's products both halfway through their completion and when they were completed.

*Project: Large, complex, global*

Brianna had to work with her key suppliers to complete the project's quality management approach. Although she could reference a lot of the information from her company's quality management system, the project was reliant on the suppliers providing quality work to agreed quality standards – especially internationally recognised standards. Because of this, appropriate references were required from the supplier organisation's quality management systems. Where there were overlaps or contradictions, the project board was called in to resolve the problems and to solidify their position.

## Quality register

> ### PURPOSE:
>
> *A quality register is used to summarise all quality management activities that are planned or have taken place, and provides information for the end-stage reports and end project report. Its purpose is to:*
>
> - *Issue a unique reference for each quality activity*
> - *Act as a pointer to the quality records for a product*
> - *Act as a summary of the number and type of quality activities undertaken.*

### When is it created? When is it updated?

- Created during the initiating a project process, when the quality management approach is defined; initial version will be blank
- Updated during the controlling a stage, managing product delivery, managing a stage boundary and closing a project processes.

### Illustration

*Project: Small, simple, local*

Quentin – fulfilling the roles of project manager, team manager and project support – used his daily log as his quality register throughout the project.

*Project: Large, complex, global*

Narinda had a bespoke database created for her project. Project support staff members were the only ones with editor access to the database. They entered in the timings of planned quality activities from the project manager's stage plans. As products were completed and tested, team managers would call into project support to inform them of the quality check results. Project support would then update the database with this new information. This system of strict control and access to the quality register ensured that no fraudulent or dishonest changes could be made to quality check results. Project assurance performed ad hoc reviews and audits of the process to ensure it worked correctly.

**Risk management approach**

### PURPOSE:

*A risk management approach describes how risks will be managed on the project. This includes the specific processes, procedures, techniques, standards and responsibilities to be applied.*

*When is it created? When is it updated?*

- Created during the initiating a project process
- If required, updated during the managing a stage boundary process.

*Illustration*

*Project: Small, simple, local*

Carla referenced her corporate risk management system and noted that, even though all her risks could be captured and assessed in her daily log, risk owners would need to be – at least – in a managerial level within the organisation.

*Project: Large, complex, global*

Kimberly referenced her organisation's comprehensive risk management strategy. Over several years, the organisation had developed a highly tuned risk strategy based on their experiences in international and highly competitive industries. Because of this investment in defining this strategy, the project had little option but to comply with it fully. Specific information about how Kimberly's project team would divide and allocate risk management activities was all that could be adjusted for this effort. All other areas required strict adherence – for example, to risk categories, scales for impact and probability, reporting requirements, etc.

**Risk register**

| PURPOSE: |
| :---: |
| *A risk register provides a record of identified risks relating to the project, including their status and history. It is used to capture and maintain information on all the identified threats and opportunities relating the project.* |

*When is it created? When is it updated?*

- Created during the initiating a project process. Any risks identified earlier will be transferred from the daily log to the risk register
- Updated during the initiating a project, controlling a stage, managing a stage boundary and closing a project processes.

## Illustration

### Project: Small, simple, local

Tomasina – fulfilling the roles of project manager, team manager and project support – used her daily log as her risk register throughout the project.

### Project: Large, complex, global

Martina's corporate risk management system served as the project's risk register. It had the functionality to assess the net present values (NPV) of risks and provide a realistic risk profile for the project. The system had been used by all the projects within the organisation and was established as being fool proof.

### Work package

---

**PURPOSE:**

*A work package is a set of information about one or more required products collated by the project manager to pass responsibility for work or delivery formally to a team manager or team member.*

---

### When is it created? When is it updated?

- Created during the controlling a stage process by the project manager
- Possibly updated in the negotiations between the project manager and team manager in the authorisation of and acceptance of the work package
- Possibly amended as a result of taking corrective action in reaction to an issue or risk.

## *Illustration*

### *Project: Small, simple, local*

Dale did not create any work packages. He was performing both the project manager and team manager roles and, therefore, didn't need the extra paperwork.

### *Project: Large, complex, global*

Zita used the company's formal contract template to delegate work to team managers. The format ensured that the work was respected and given the attention it deserved, even from internal team managers. She required the team managers to sign and date the work packages when they accepted them. Copies of the work packages were also sent to the team managers' line managers, so that they fully understood the work their staff member was undertaking. For external team managers, Zita would issue formal feedback upon her work package status reviews. This, again, showed the suppliers how serious she was in managing and remaining in tight control over the project's work.

# ITG RESOURCES

IT Governance Ltd sources, creates and delivers products and services to meet the real-world, evolving IT governance needs of today's organisations, directors, managers and practitioners.

The ITG website (*www.itgovernance.co.uk*) is the international one-stop-shop for corporate and IT governance information, advice, guidance, books, tools, training and consultancy. On the website you will find the following page related to the subject matter of this book:

*www.itgovernance.co.uk/prince2*

## Publishing Services

IT Governance Publishing (ITGP) is the world's leading IT-GRC publishing imprint that is wholly owned by IT Governance Ltd.

With books and tools covering all IT governance, risk and compliance frameworks, we are the publisher of choice for authors and distributors alike, producing unique and practical publications of the highest quality, in the latest formats available, which readers will find invaluable.

*www.itgovernancepublishing.co.uk* is the website dedicated to ITGP. Other titles published by ITGP that may be of interest include:

- PRINCE2 Agile™ An Implementation Pocket Guide
  *www.itgovernance.co.uk/shop/product/prince2-agile-an-implementation-pocket-guide-step-by-step-advice-for-every-project-type*
- Everything you want to know about Agile
  *www.itgovernance.co.uk/shop/product/everything-you-want-to-know-about-agile*

- The Power of the Agile Business Analyst
  *www.itgovernance.co.uk/shop/product/the-power-of-the-agile-business-analyst*

We also offer a range of toolkits that give comprehensive, customisable documents to help users create the specific documentation they need to properly implement a management system or standard. Written by experienced practitioners and based on the latest best practice, ITGP toolkits can save months of work for organisations working towards compliance with a given standard.

Please visit *www.itgovernance.co.uk/shop/category/itgp-toolkits* to see our full range of toolkits.

Books and tools published by IT Governance Publishing (ITGP) are available from all business booksellers and the following websites:

*www.itgovernance.eu*    *www.itgovernanceusa.com*

*www.itgovernance.asia* *www.itgovernancegulf.com*

**Training Services**

IT Governance offers an extensive portfolio of training courses designed to educate information security, IT governance, risk management and compliance professionals. Our classroom and online training programmes will help you develop the skills required to deliver best practice and compliance to your organisation. They will also enhance your career by providing you with industry standard certifications and increased peer recognition. Our range of courses offer a structured learning path from Foundation to Advanced level in the key topics of information security, IT governance, business continuity and service management.

Full details of all IT Governance training courses can be found at *www.itgovernance.co.uk/training.aspx*.

## Consultancy services

The IT Governance consultancy team can show you how to apply PRINCE2 concepts to the most complex development projects. Our expert consultants can guide and inspire you in the use of project management, providing you with the practical techniques to improve delivery efficiencies, control your implementation costs, and meet your sales targets by building customer loyalty.

We will show you the project management methods that create flexibility and ensure adaptability to changing circumstances, accepting that nothing changes more than your customer's needs. You will learn how to change from a traditional hierarchy towards self-empowered individuals and teams. In this way, you will develop engaged employees with the responsibility, accountability and authority to deliver to the customer's requirements, shaping and directing outcomes, while regularly delivering partial, though functional, products.

For more information about IT Governance consultancy services see *www.itgovernance.co.uk/consulting.aspx*.

## Daily Sentinel

Want to stay up-to-date with the latest developments and resources in the IT GRC market? We will send you mobile-friendly emails with fresh news and features about your preferred areas of interest, as well as unmissable offers and free resources to help you successfully start your projects.

*www.itgovernance.co.uk/daily-sentinel*

**Branded Publishing Services**

ITGP's wide range of titles provide information governance, risk management and compliance (IT GRC) expertise from renowned industry practitioners.

If you're taking advantage of our expert knowledge in your organisation, you can now customise our titles with your own branding thanks to our Branded Publishing Service. For more information, please visit *www.itgovernancepublishing.co.uk/publishing-services.aspx*.

EU for product safety is Stephen Evans, The Mill Enterprise Hub, Stagreenan, Drogheda, Co. Louth, A92 CD3D, Ireland. (servicecentre@itgovernance.eu)

www.ingramcontent.com/pod-product-compliance
Lightning Source LLC
Chambersburg PA
CBHW071108050326
40690CB00008B/1160